SHARING CHRIST'S PRIESTHOOD

SHARING CHRIST'S PRIESTHOOD

A Bible Study for Catholics

by MIKE AQUILINA

Our Sunday Visitor Publishing Division
Our Sunday Visitor, Inc.
Huntington, Indiana 46750

Nihil Obstat: Rev. Michael Heintz, Ph.D., *Censor Librorum*
Imprimatur: ✠ John M. D'Arcy
Bishop of Fort Wayne-South Bend
July 28, 2009

The *Nihil Obstat* and *Imprimatur* are official declarations that a book or pamphlet is free of doctrinal or moral error. No implication is contained therein that those who have granted the *Nihil Obstat* or *Imprimatur* agree with the contents, opinions, or statements expressed.

The Scripture citations used in this work are taken from the *Second Catholic Edition of the Revised Standard Version of the Bible* (RSV), copyright © 1965, 1966, and 2006 by the Division of Christian Education of the National Council of the Churches of Christ in the United States of America. Used by permission. All rights reserved.

English translation of the *Catechism of the Catholic Church for the United States of America*, copyright © 1994, United States Catholic Conference, Inc. — Libreria Editrice Vaticana. English translation of the *Catechism of the Catholic Church: Modifications from the Editio Typica*, copyright © 1997, United States Catholic Conference, Inc. — Libreria Editrice Vaticana.

Every reasonable effort has been made to determine copyright holders of excerpted materials and to secure permissions as needed. If any copyrighted materials have been inadvertently used in this work without proper credit being given in one form or another, please notify Our Sunday Visitor in writing so that future printings of this work may be corrected accordingly.

Our Sunday Visitor Publishing Division
Our Sunday Visitor, Inc., 200 Noll Plaza, Huntington, IN 46750
1-800-348-2440
bookpermissions@osv.com

ISBN: 1-59276-678-9 (Inventory No. T957)
LCCN: 2009931096

Cover design by Lindsey Luken / Cover image: The Crosiers
Interior design by Sherri L. Hoffman

PRINTED IN THE UNITED STATES OF AMERICA

DEDICATION

Dedicated to the memory of my friends,
Fr. Ronald Lawler, O.F.M. Cap.,
Fr. Joseph Linck,
and Fr. Leopold Krul, O.S.B.,
priests forever and teachers of priests.

Contents

Introduction: What Is a Priest?   9

A Note to Readers   10

Leading a Discussion   11

SESSION 1: The Natural Priesthood   13

SESSION 2: Priesthood under the Law   29

SESSION 3: Jesus, the Great High Priest   47

SESSION 4: We the Priests   55

SESSION 5: The Priesthood of the Apostles   65

SESSION 6: The Biblical Priesthood Today   79

For Further Reading   95

What Is a Priest?

That, of course, is what this whole study is about. But here's a quick answer:

A priest is someone who stands as a mediator between God and humanity.

Priests offer sacrifices to God on behalf of the people. Hebrews 5:1 gives us a simple description of what a priest does: "For every high priest chosen from among men is appointed to act on behalf of men in relation to God, to offer gifts and sacrifices for sins."

Catholics see several levels of priesthood.

- First, we are all priests. Every believer has a direct relationship with Jesus Christ, who is God.
- Second, Jesus Christ is our great high priest. Because he is both God and man, he is the mediator between us and God the Father.
- Third, we have an ordained priesthood: men who have devoted their lives to the service of God, and who have been sacramentally marked as belonging to God.

These are not conflicting ideas of priesthood: they're all aspects of the same thing. There are girls, boys, men, and women, but we're all equally human. There are lay believers, priests, bishops, and Christ himself — all priests, but different aspects of the priesthood.

Everything the Church teaches about the priesthood has its roots in the Bible, and that's what this study is about. We'll look at all three kinds of priesthood: the ordained priesthood, the common priesthood, and the priesthood of Christ. We'll see how the priesthood developed through salvation history, and how Christ ultimately restored the primitive priesthood that Adam was meant to have.

That's why we're beginning at the beginning of everything: the creation of the world.

A Note to Readers

This Bible study is intended for both private use and for group discussion. Questions are provided both to help you grasp the meaning of the Scripture texts and to expand your understanding of the nature of priesthood. Each chapter ends with "In Practice" questions designed to help you apply the biblical message to your life.

Leading a Discussion

Study groups come in all sizes, with all different kinds of people. Even where you meet has a big effect on how the group works: meeting in a coffee shop feels a lot more informal than meeting in a conference room. There's no one set of rules that fits every circumstance, so anything you read here should be taken as a suggestion only.

If you're leading discussions, here are some general suggestions:

1. Keep it friendly.

An informal setting works best, especially for smaller groups. If the study group feels like a conversation among friends, people will want to keep coming. If it feels like a committee meeting, people may find excuses to stay away.

2. Try to get everyone talking.

Don't badger people who seem to be quiet, but do try to involve them personally in the conversation. Ask them for opinions; don't put them on the spot with questions that seem like tests.

3. Make room for short digressions.

If something you're talking about reminds somebody of a personal story, that's fine. It's good when people can relate personally to the subject. However...

4. Always bring the conversation back to the topic.

Don't let it stray too far from what you're talking about. If someone seems to have strayed a bit, try to find something relevant in what he or she just said and use it to bring the conversation back on course.

The Natural Priesthood

BEFORE YOU START . . .

Read Genesis, chapters 1 and 2.

After you've read those two chapters, look back at the reading and think about these questions. You can write down your answers here. Feel free to change them as you read on (use pencil to make this easier!). This isn't a test: it's just meant to help you gather your thoughts so that you can discuss them with other people in your session.

How many times does the creation narrative say that "God saw that it was good"?	
In chapter 1, what is the very last thing God creates?	
At the end of the sixth day, when God saw everything he had made, how was God's reaction different from before?	
In 2:15, what was the man supposed to do in the garden?	

CREATED GOOD

In his book *Swear to God,* Scott Hahn helpfully divides human history into three periods:

1. The age of nature, from creation to the Exodus from Egypt.
2. The age of law, from the Exodus to the birth of Jesus Christ.
3. The age of grace, from the coming of Christ up to now.

Each age has its own particular kind of priesthood. In this session, we're going to look at the priesthood of the age of nature: what we might call the *natural priesthood.*

We know that God created Adam and Eve to live in perfect happiness, knowing God himself intimately, and seeing him face-to-face. God speaks to both of them directly. There's no mediator between Adam and God.

In the very beginning, God assigned the man and the woman to take care of the rest of his creation. You read this passage at the beginning, but let's look at it closely now:

GENESIS 1

[26]Then God said, "Let us make man in our image, after our likeness; and let them have dominion over the fish of the sea, and over the birds of the air, and over the cattle, and over all the earth, and over every creeping thing that creeps upon the earth." [27]So God created man in his own image, in the image of God he created him; male and female he created them. [28]And God blessed them, and God said to them, "Be fruitful and multiply, and fill the earth and subdue it; and have dominion over the fish of the sea and over the birds of the air and over every living thing that moves upon the earth." [29]And God said, "Behold, I have given you every plant yielding seed which is upon the face of all the earth, and every tree with seed in its fruit; you shall have them for food. [30]And to every beast of the earth, and to every bird of the air, and to everything that creeps on the earth, everything that has the breath of life, I have given every green plant for food." And it was so.

Look back at this reading and think about these questions. You can write down your answers here. Feel free to change them as you read on.

What do you think it means for man and woman to be created "in the image of God"?	
The familiar story of Eve's being made from Adam's rib comes later. By saying only that "male and female he created them," what does this narrative emphasize about our relationship with God?	
What does it mean for humans to "have dominion over" the rest of creation? Is it ours to do with as we like?	

THE PRIEST OF EDEN

Living in paradise didn't mean a life with no duties. When Genesis 2 describes in detail how the first man was created, it tells us that God gave him a very specific duty:

> The LORD God took the man and put him in the garden of Eden to till it and keep it.
>
> — GENESIS 2:15

The word "till" makes Adam sound like a farmer, and certainly we know it was his duty to "have dominion over" the plants and animals of Eden. But the only other places in the Bible where we find the Hebrew words we translate as "till" and "keep" are in Numbers, where they describe the liturgical duties of the Levites — the priestly tribe of Israel.

Adam, in other words, is meant to be a priest in God's temple, which is the Garden of Eden — and, in fact, all of creation.

That helps us understand what kind of "dominion" Adam and Eve were supposed to have over the earth. God wasn't telling them to do whatever they wanted to his creation; God was telling them to be mediators. Adam and Eve were meant to be the priests who mediated between God and creation, seeing that God's will was done on Earth as it is in heaven.

Of course, as we know, they failed.

Because Adam and Eve were the mediators between God and creation, their sin corrupted all creation. It broke the perfect world they were meant to live in. More importantly, it broke the perfectly intimate relationship they were meant to have with God.

So Adam was, in a sense, defrocked as priest of Eden. But he and his descendants would still have to maintain a relationship with God somehow.

OFFERINGS TO THE LORD

Expelled from Eden, Adam and Eve have two sons, Cain and Abel. The first thing we hear about them is how they offered sacrifices to God. But Cain's sacrifice was not acceptable:

GENESIS 4

[1]Now Adam knew Eve his wife, and she conceived and bore Cain, saying, "I have gotten a man with the help of the LORD." [2]And again, she bore his brother Abel. Now Abel was a keeper of sheep, and Cain a tiller of the ground. [3]In the course of time Cain brought to the Lord an offering of the fruit of the ground, [4]and Abel brought of the firstlings of his flock and of their fat portions. And the Lord had regard for Abel and his offering, [5]but for Cain and his offering he had no regard. So Cain was very angry, and his countenance fell. [6]The LORD said to Cain, "Why are you angry, and why has your countenance fallen? [7]If you do well, will you not be accepted?

And if you do not do well, sin is lurking at the door; its desire is for you, but you must master it."

This is the first time we hear of someone offering sacrifices to God, and it comes *immediately* after the expulsion from Eden. Some questions to think about:

Why do we hear about sacrifices as soon as Adam and Eve have been expelled from Eden?	
How has our relationship with God changed?	
Why does God say Cain's sacrifice wasn't accepted?	

There are no professional priests to offer sacrifices. Instead, every man offers his own sacrifice to God. Our relationship with God is broken, but there's still no better way — no mediator stands between us and God.

Throughout the time of the patriarchs, the ancient ancestors of Israel whose lives are chronicled in Genesis, the people of God will have no separate class of priests. But we'll begin to see a familiar family pattern emerging: the *father* of the family makes sacrifices for his whole household. So, for example, after the Flood, when the land is dry again, Noah makes an offering for his whole family:

GENESIS 8

¹⁵Then God said to Noah, ¹⁶"Go forth from the ark, you and your wife, and your sons and your sons' wives with you. ¹⁷Bring forth with you every living thing that is with you of all flesh — birds and

---

IS GENESIS TRUE?

When we talk about the early chapters of Genesis, people sometimes get a bit nervous. Did God really create the world in seven literal days? Did it all happen only a few thousand years ago? To be Christian, do we have to reject what modern science claims about the universe?

Sometimes we'd rather sweep Genesis under the rug than deal with these questions. But they don't need to cause us unnecessary worry.

For a Catholic, the exact mechanism of creation is not the important question. Science is a fascinating and useful tool for discovering how the world around us works. But Scripture is meant to teach us moral and religious truths.

The Church doesn't require Catholics to believe in any particular theory of the origin of the universe. It's not important to faith or morals exactly when, or how, the world came together.

What the Church does teach, and we must believe, is much more important:

1. That God is responsible for the whole created universe.
2. That it was created good.
3. That human beings were specially created to know God.
4. That, through our sin, we broke that intimate relationship.
5. That God had planned our salvation from the beginning, and accomplished it through his Son, Jesus Christ.

Genesis teaches us the important truths of creation. We're free to believe the most plausible scientific theories about the origin of the universe and created beings — or to take the Genesis account completely literally. What we need to learn from Genesis concerns our faith, not science.

animals and every creeping thing that creeps on the earth — that they may breed abundantly on the earth, and be fruitful and multiply upon the earth." ¹⁸So Noah went forth, and his sons and his wife and his sons' wives with him. ¹⁹And every beast, every creeping thing, and every bird, everything that moves upon the earth, went forth by families out of the ark.

²⁰Then Noah built an altar to the LORD, and took of every clean animal and of every clean bird, and offered burnt offerings on the altar. ²¹And when the LORD smelled the pleasing odor, the Lord said in his heart, "I will never again curse the ground because of man, for the imagination of man's heart is evil from his youth; neither will I ever again destroy every living creature as I have done. ²²While the earth remains, seedtime and harvest, cold and heat, summer and winter, day and night, shall not cease."

Some questions to think about:

How is Noah like Adam at this point?	
What preparations does Noah have to make to offer his sacrifice?	
For whom does Noah offer his sacrifice?	

Why does the Lord decide not to "curse the ground" again? Is it because sin has been eliminated in the Flood?	

Noah and his family are the only humans left in all creation, and here we see Noah acting as a priest for all creation. The story shows Noah's sacrifice as interceding with God, not just for his family, but for every living thing. In a sense, he is filling the role Adam was meant to fill as a priest for all creation.

We can also see something about the *kind* of worship Noah was offering. God spoke directly to Noah, but Noah still built an altar and made sacrifices. There was a particular ritual associated with this kind of worship. Noah had to gather materials, build an altar in a particular way, and offer sacrifices of *clean* animals — animals that were suitable for ritual sacrifice.

In other words, in spite of his intimate relationship with God, Noah didn't just make it up as he went along. His worship was *liturgical* — it followed a specific form.

But, of course, Noah broke his relationship with God, just as Adam had done before him. His drunkenness tore his family apart, and evil continued its course in the world. But the line of Noah's son Shem, though far from perfect, would stay faithful to God. Ten generations from Noah, we come to Abraham.

ABRAHAM, THE FRIEND OF GOD

In Genesis 12, we read how God told Abram (the future Abraham) to pick up and move to Canaan, a place he had never seen before. There, God would make a great nation out of Abram.

So Abram picked up his family and moved with his whole household, and when he arrived in Canaan, God appeared to tell him that this was the place.

GENESIS 12

[1]Now the LORD said to Abram, "Go from your country and your kindred and your father's house to the land that I will show you. [2]And I will make of you a great nation, and I will bless you, and make your name great, so that you will be a blessing. [3]I will bless those who bless you, and him who curses you I will curse; and by you all the families of the earth shall bless themselves."

[4]So Abram went, as the LORD had told him; and Lot went with him. Abram was seventy-five years old when he departed from Haran. [5]And Abram took Sarai his wife, and Lot his brother's son, and all their possessions which they had gathered, and the persons that they had gotten in Haran; and they set forth to go to the land of Canaan. When they had come to the land of Canaan, [6]Abram passed through the land to the place at Shechem, to the oak of Moreh. At that time the Canaanites were in the land. [7]Then the LORD appeared to Abram, and said, "To your descendants I will give this land." So he built there an altar to the LORD, who had appeared to him. [8]Thence he removed to the mountain on the east of Bethel, and pitched his tent, with Bethel on the west and Ai on the east; and there he built an altar to the LORD and called on the name of the LORD.

Some questions to think about:

What kind of faith did it take for Abram to uproot himself this way?	
What is the first thing Abram does when he arrives in Canaan?	

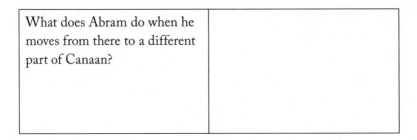

What does Abram do when he moves from there to a different part of Canaan?	

Abram builds an altar to offer sacrifice to God, who speaks to him directly. We see him acting as a priest for himself, his family, and his extended household.

In fact, we'll see Abraham — as he will be called once he settles in Canaan — taking on the role of mediator between God and humanity more than once.

One of the best-known stories in Abraham's life is the story of his negotiating with God over Sodom. The wickedness of the Sodomites had brought on God's wrath, and he intended to destroy the place. In Genesis 18:23-33, we read how Abraham bargained with God.

GENESIS 18

[23]Then Abraham drew near, and said, "Will you indeed destroy the righteous with the wicked? [24]Suppose there are fifty righteous within the city; will you then destroy the place and not spare it for the fifty righteous who are in it? [25]Far be it from you to do such a thing, to slay the righteous with the wicked, so that the righteous fare as the wicked! Far be that from you! Shall not the Judge of all the earth do right?" [26]And the LORD said, "If I find at Sodom fifty righteous in the city, I will spare the whole place for their sake."

Having gained that point, Abraham went on to talk God down to forty-five, and then forty, bargaining as if he were dealing with a merchant in a bazaar. He finally talked God down to ten.

The story has a touch of humor about it, albeit of the dark variety. But it also shows us Abram taking on one of the main duties of a priest. He *mediates* between God and the people of Sodom.

You'll notice that the mediation didn't save the people from the consequence of their sin. Abraham as priest couldn't save them by himself; they would have needed to cooperate by repenting. But Abraham did all a priest could do.

Throughout the story of Abraham, we see him building altars and offering sacrifices. But the most famous story of Abraham is the story of the sacrifice he *didn't* offer.

GENESIS 22

[1]After these things God tested Abraham, and said to him, "Abraham!" And he said, "Here am I." [2]He said, "Take your son, your only son Isaac, whom you love, and go to the land of Moriah, and offer him there as a burnt offering upon one of the mountains of which I shall tell you." [3]So Abraham rose early in the morning, saddled his ass, and took two of his young men with him, and his son Isaac; and he cut the wood for the burnt offering, and arose and went to the place of which God had told him. [4]On the third day Abraham lifted up his eyes and saw the place afar off. [5]Then Abraham said to his young men, "Stay here with the ass; I and the lad will go yonder and worship, and come again to you." [6]And Abraham took the wood of the burnt offering, and laid it on Isaac his son; and he took in his hand the fire and the knife. So they went both of them together. [7]And Isaac said to his father Abraham, "My father!" And he said, "Here am I, my son." He said, "Behold, the fire and the wood; but where is the lamb for a burnt offering?" [8]Abraham said, "God will provide himself the lamb for a burnt offering, my son." So they went both of them together.

[9]When they came to the place of which God had told him, Abraham built an altar there, and laid the wood in order, and bound Isaac his son, and laid him on the altar, upon the wood. [10]Then Abraham put forth his hand, and took the knife to slay his son. [11]But the angel of the LORD called to him from heaven, and said, "Abraham, Abraham!" And he said, "Here am I." [12]He said, "Do not lay your hand on the lad or do anything to him; for now I know that you fear God, seeing you have not withheld your son, your only son, from me." [13]And Abraham lifted up his eyes and looked, and behold, behind him was a ram, caught in a thicket by his horns; and Abraham went and took the ram, and offered it

up as a burnt offering instead of his son. [14]So Abraham called the name of that place The LORD will provide; as it is said to this day, "On the mount of the LORD it shall be provided."

Some questions to think about:

How old do you think Isaac was? Was he a little child or a young man? To answer this question, consider your answer to the next:	
Who carried the wood for the sacrifice?	
Could Isaac have gotten away if he wanted to?	
What story in the New Testament does this remind you of?	

The Binding of Isaac is the story that defines Abraham. He had such trust in God that he was willing to sacrifice his own son if that was what God required. And this story that defines Abraham is a story of him acting as a priest, preparing to offer a sacrifice to God.

There's much more significance to the story. We'll see later on that Moriah, the hill on which Isaac was to be offered, became the very center of worship for the people of God.

MELCHIZEDEK, PRIEST OF GOD MOST HIGH

So far, we've been looking at Abraham acting as a priest, with a direct relationship to God. But there is one incident where Abraham meets another priest. In fact, it's the first time in the Bible we see somebody referred to as a "priest."

It happened early in Abraham's stay in Canaan, while he was still known as Abram. A king named Cherdolaomer, with his allies, had ransacked Sodom and the area around it, carrying off everything valuable and taking captives. When Abram heard that his nephew Lot was among the captives, he gathered his tribe together and defeated Cherdolaomer to rescue Lot. On his return, we hear, he was greeted by two kings:

GENESIS 14

[17]After his return from the defeat of Chedorlaomer and the kings who were with him, the king of Sodom went out to meet him at the Valley of Shaveh (that is, the King's Valley). [18]And Melchizedek king of Salem brought out bread and wine; he was priest of God Most High. [19]And he blessed him and said,

> "Blessed be Abram by God Most High,
>> maker of heaven and earth;
> [20]and blessed be God Most High,
>> who has delivered your enemies into your hand!"

Here are two questions to help us look at that passage carefully, because the writers of the New Testament considered it one of the most important things in the Hebrew Scriptures:

What two positions does Melchizedek hold?	
What two things does he bring out to Abram?	

Melchizedek is king of Salem, a city whose name means "peace." It's an old name for the city we know as Jerusalem. He is also a priest of God Most High — long before any of Abraham's descendants became priests.

Otherwise, we really don't know anything about him. We don't know when he was born, when he died, who his parents were, who his descendants were, or anything else about him.

But the very mystery of Melchizedek made him a powerful and important figure in the idea of the priesthood. He was not of the tribe of Levi, which would later become the priestly tribe in Israel. In fact, he was not even an Israelite. Psalm 110 uses his example to describe the position of the Lord's Anointed, the coming Messiah:

PSALM 110

[4]The LORD has sworn
and will not change his mind,
"You are a priest for ever
after the order of Melchizedek."

Why Melchizedek? His unique position as a non-Israelite priest of the true God looks forward to the time when all nations, not just Israel, will come to know God.

The letter to the Hebrews develops the idea of Melchizedek as predecessor to the Messiah, finding the real meaning of Melchizedek in that very mystery that surrounds him.

HEBREWS 7

[1]For this Melchizedek, king of Salem, priest of the Most High God, met Abraham returning from the slaughter of the kings and blessed him; [2]and to him Abraham apportioned a tenth part of everything. He is first, by translation of his name, king of righteousness, and then he is also king of Salem, that is, king of peace. [3]He is without father or mother or genealogy, and has neither beginning of days nor end of life, but resembling the Son of God he continues a priest for ever.

[4]See how great he is! Abraham the patriarch gave him a tithe of the spoils. [5]And those descendants of Levi who receive the priestly office have a commandment in the law to take tithes from the people, that is, from their brethren, though these also are descended from Abraham. [6]But this man who has not their genealogy received tithes from Abraham and blessed him who had the promises. [7]It is beyond dispute that the inferior is blessed by the superior.

Melchizedek was a priest superior to Abraham, and his priesthood resembles the priesthood of the Son of God. Later on, we'll see just what this identification with Melchizedek implies.

THE NATION OF ISRAEL BEGINS

Abraham's descendants continued to build altars for their own worship. We see Abraham's son, Isaac, and his son, Jacob, building altars for their own worship. Jacob, of course, was given the new name Israel, and his twelve sons would be the ancestors of the twelve tribes of that great nation God promised to Abraham.

But as they prospered and grew more numerous, they were being prepared for their special role in God's plan to save humanity from our own sin.

God had promised that all nations would be blessed through Abraham; soon, we'll see the next stage in the fulfillment of that promise.

IN PRACTICE . . .

Think back to the story of creation, and how Adam and Eve were given dominion over all creation.

What part of creation is most directly your responsibility?

- Think of your family, your pets, your house, your yard (and everything that grows in it), your vote in the next election. How are you responsible for those parts of creation?
- How do you exercise your dominion over them?
- What do you think was God's plan in putting you in charge of that part of his universe?
- When you think about your responsibilities that way, does it suggest any changes in how you take care of your part of the world?

Write down some of your ideas here, and you can talk about them with the other people in your session.

Priesthood under the Law

BEFORE YOU START . . .

Read Exodus, chapter 19.

After you've read that chapter, look back at the reading and think about these questions. You can write down your answers here. Feel free to change them as you read on.

Where does this chapter take place? What is that place famous for?	
What kind of kingdom does God promise that Israel will be?	
What conditions does that promise depend on? What does Israel have to do?	

WHY THE EXODUS?

The book of Exodus opens generations after the end of Genesis. The descendants of Israel (that is, Jacob) had prospered and multiplied into a great nation, but a xenophobic pharaoh had enslaved them. It was time for the next stage in the plan of redemption: the deliverance of Israel from Egypt, and the giving of the Law.

We all remember the story of the Exodus from Egypt — the ten plagues, the dramatic escape across the sea, the pillar of cloud and fire. But what was the purpose of that astonishing divine intervention? The Egyptians were treating the Israelites badly, but people have been treated badly all over the world since Cain killed Abel. There must have been more to it than that.

And so there was. God had promised that all the nations of the world would be blessed through Abraham. The Exodus was the next stage in the fulfillment of that promise.

In fact, when they reached Sinai, God told the Israelites explicitly what he expected to do with them.

Exodus 19

⁴"You have seen what I did to the Egyptians, and how I bore you on eagles' wings and brought you to myself. ⁵Now therefore, if you will obey my voice and keep my covenant, you shall be my own possession among all peoples; for all the earth is mine, ⁶and you shall be to me a kingdom of priests and a holy nation."

That was the purpose of the Exodus: not simply to rescue an unjustly enslaved people, but to make them into a kingdom of priests.

Remember our definition of a priest: a priest is someone who stands as a mediator between God and humanity. That was the position Israel was being given. Through Israel, his holy nation, God would reach out to the rest of humanity. As God reminded them, all the earth belonged to him, but now they would belong to him in a unique way.

Here are some questions to think about. You can write down your answers here. Feel free to change them as you read on.

Why did God need a nation of priests?	
Why wouldn't God choose some respectable nation, like the Egyptians, whose power was the envy of the rest of the world? Why choose a people who had nothing and got no respect from anyone?	
Why is obeying the covenant a necessary condition of being a kingdom of priests?	

NOT READY TO BE PRIESTS

At Sinai, God gave Israel the Ten Commandments — the fundamental laws by which they would live as a nation. But even before Moses was finished on Sinai, the Israelites had lost patience with him. They forced Aaron to make them a "golden calf" — something like the idols they had been familiar with in Egypt (Exodus 32:1-6). Then they worshiped that as if it were the god who had brought them out of bondage!

They were not ready to be priests. They had taken the priesthood God gave to them, alone out of all the nations of the earth, and offered it to a golden idol made from their castoff jewelry.

To avert the complete destruction of the people that God had threatened, Moses meted out a harsh punishment:

EXODUS 32

[25]And when Moses saw that the people had broken loose (for Aaron had let them break loose, to their shame among their enemies), [26]then Moses stood in the gate of the camp, and said, "Who is on the LORD's side? Come to me." And all the sons of Levi gathered themselves together to him. [27]And he said to them, "Thus says the LORD God of Israel, 'Put every man his sword on his side, and go to and fro from gate to gate throughout the camp, and slay every man his brother, and every man his companion, and every man his neighbor.'" [28]And the sons of Levi did according to the word of Moses; and there fell of the people that day about three thousand men. [29]And Moses said, "Today you have ordained yourselves for the service of the LORD, each one at the cost of his son and of his brother, that he may bestow a blessing upon you this day."

THE ORGY OF THE GOLDEN CALF

When we say that Israel "worshiped" the golden calf, we don't do justice to what Moses saw when he came down the mountain after his forty days on Sinai.

God had already informed him of what the Israelites were up to, and he pleaded with God to spare them (Exodus 32:7-14). He knew they had turned away from God.

So he should have been prepared for what he saw when he came down from Sinai, if all the people were doing was praying to a golden idol.

Instead, what he saw made him so furious that he threw the stone tablets down and shattered them in pieces — the tablets on which God himself had written the Law. The people "sat down to eat and drink, and rose up to play." Moses heard singing and saw dancing. In other words, the people were celebrating a pagan fertility rite, which was an excuse for a wild orgy — the bull or "calf" being a common symbol of fertility.

These were the people who were supposed to be God's holy nation!

The sons of Levi — the Levites, as we call the tribe to which Moses belonged — were the ones who declared themselves on the side of the true God. This bloody "ordination" set them aside as the priestly tribe in Israel; they would be the mediators between God and the rest of Israel.

The kingdom of priests would need a tribe of priests.

Why was the Israelites' lapse so horrible? We should remember where they had come from and where they were going.

Egypt was a land of many gods — hundreds, even thousands, of them. Often, the worship of these gods involved just the sort of immorality the Israelites had committed at the base of Mount Sinai. The whole country was a school of idolatry, where the Israelites had learned to look for gods in animal form around every corner.

But Canaan, the land they were headed for, was worse. There also, the people worshiped many gods, but orgies were the least of their gods' demands. Women and men were forced into prostitution by the demands of the Canaanite gods. Most horrible of all were the gods who demanded human sacrifice — especially Molech, who demanded every firstborn child to be burned alive on his altar.

These monsters were the gods of the people who would surround Israel, and history would prove that the Israelites were constantly open to the temptations of these frightful false gods. This is why the prophets of Israel always attacked even the smallest lapse into idolatry as a dreadful sin. But what Moses had seen at the base of Sinai went far beyond a small lapse. God's own people were embracing the worst kind of pagan impurity with gusto.

THE CEREMONIAL LAW

After Exodus come three more books filled with laws: Leviticus, Numbers, and Deuteronomy. These laws regulate practically everything the people of Israel do, from what they eat to how they dress.

Why so many regulations? Why was it necessary to prescribe so many rituals and to spell out so many prohibitions?

The answer is in that golden calf the people made while Moses was up on Mount Sinai. The Israelites were chosen by God to be his own holy nation, but they had shown that, left to themselves, they would be distracted by the first shiny object they stumbled across... so they couldn't be left to themselves. They needed a babysitter.

That's the way St. Paul describes it in his letter to the Galatians. God had promised to bless all nations through Abraham. That promise, made long before Moses brought the Law down from the mountain, was not made invalid by the Law; rather, the Law was our "custodian" — a word that, in Greek, referred to a servant put in charge of the master's children.

GALATIANS 3

[16]Now the promises were made to Abraham and to his offspring. It does not say, "And to offsprings," referring to many; but, referring to one, "And to your offspring," which is Christ. [17]This is what I mean: the law, which came four hundred and thirty years afterward, does not annul a covenant previously ratified by God, so as to make the promise void. [18]For if the inheritance is by the law, it is no longer by promise; but God gave it to Abraham by a promise.

[19]Why then the law? It was added because of transgressions, till the offspring should come to whom the promise had been made; and it was ordained by angels through an intermediary. [20]Now an intermediary implies more than one; but God is one.

[21]Is the law then against the promises of God? Certainly not; for if a law had been given which could make alive, then righteousness would indeed be by the law. [22]But the scripture consigned all things to sin, that what was promised to faith in Jesus Christ might be given to those who believe.

[23]Now before faith came, we were confined under the law, kept under restraint until faith should be revealed. [24]So that the law was our custodian until Christ came, that we might be justified by faith. [25]But now that faith has come, we are no longer under a custodian; [26]for in Christ Jesus you are all sons of God, through faith. [27]For as many of you as were baptized into Christ have put on Christ. [28]There is neither Jew nor Greek, there is neither slave nor free, there is neither male nor female; for you are all one in Christ

Jesus. [29]And if you are Christ's, then you are Abraham's offspring, heirs according to promise.

Some questions to think about on this reading:

Is following the Law the way we claim the inheritance promised to Abraham?	
Does the Law change the promise God made to Abraham?	
Now that Christ has come, who are the heirs of Abraham?	

How did this Law work, then? With all its minute regulations and prescriptions, the Law of Moses would teach the Israelites the holiness they didn't naturally practice. It would make them a distinct people, set apart by their diet and dress from the other nations around them.

The Law would enforce upright living, because the people couldn't be trusted to find their own way. It would enforce ritual cleanness as a constant reminder of the need for personal holiness.

It was cumbersome and difficult, but that very difficulty was what would set the people of Israel apart as God's own holy nation. It would even earn them the grudging admiration of the nations, as one conqueror after another looked at the Israelites and was amazed by the things they did for the love of their God.

THE SACRIFICIAL CULT

Above all the minute regulations that guided the life of every Israelite was the great sacrificial liturgy of Israel.

Sacrifices were prescribed for every occasion: for morning and evening, for holy days, and for important events in the life of every Israelite. Many of these were animal sacrifices, and you might notice an interesting and important detail:

The Israelites were instructed to sacrifice exactly the animals that their neighbors worshiped as gods.

Think what a powerful image that must have been! The Egyptians worshiped a bull-god. The Canaanites surrounding Israel worshiped a bull-god. When the Israelites lost patience with Moses and decided to make themselves a god they could see, the first thing they thought of was a bull-god like the ones their neighbors worshiped.

Now they were, in effect, killing that false god on their altars every day!

Sin offerings were a big part of this sacrificial cult. There were so many regulations in the Law that everyone was bound to break some of them. In fact, the Law itself took into account the fact that the people might break the rules without meaning to do it:

LEVITICUS 4

¹³"If the whole congregation of Israel commits a sin unwittingly and the thing is hidden from the eyes of the assembly, and they do any one of the things which the Lord has commanded not to be done and are guilty; ¹⁴when the sin which they have committed becomes known, the assembly shall offer a young bull for a sin offering and bring it before the tent of meeting; ¹⁵and the elders of the congregation shall lay their hands upon the head of the bull before the LORD, and the bull shall be killed before the LORD. ¹⁶Then the anointed priest shall bring some of the blood of the bull to the tent of meeting, ¹⁷and the priest shall dip his finger in the blood and sprinkle it seven times before the LORD in front of the veil. ¹⁸And he shall put some of the blood on the horns of the altar which is in the tent of meeting before the LORD; and the rest of

the blood he shall pour out at the base of the altar of burnt offering which is at the door of the tent of meeting. [19]And all its fat he shall take from it and burn upon the altar. [20]Thus shall he do with the bull; as he did with the bull of the sin offering, so shall he do with this; and the priest shall make atonement for them, and they shall be forgiven."

Some questions to help us examine the reading closely:

Does the law assume that the people intentionally sinned?	
When is the sacrifice supposed to be offered?	
Who makes the atonement for the congregation?	

If all the people sin together, they must offer a bull as sacrifice. Notice that the *priest*, not the people, performs the ritual on their behalf, standing as a mediator between them and God.

Almost the same ritual is prescribed if a priest sins unwittingly (Leviticus 4:1-12), or if a ruler sins unwittingly (Leviticus 4:22-26): a bull is sacrificed for the sin, with one of the priests performing the ritual. If one of the common people sins unwittingly, again the same ritual is prescribed (Leviticus 4:27-31), but with a goat, since one of the common people probably couldn't afford a bull.

These are just the sins the people couldn't help committing — sins where, with the best of intentions, they accidentally crossed one of the many lines drawn by the Law of Moses.

Then, of course, there are the sins we commit when we ought to know better. The Law catalogues every kind of sin and prescribes exactly the penalty for it. For the ordinary sins like rash oaths or touching unclean things, once again, a sin offering is prescribed.

It's an endless round of offerings because, of course, we're all sinners. No matter how many times the sin offerings were made, they never were enough.

HEBREWS 10

[1]For since the law has but a shadow of the good things to come instead of the true form of these realities, it can never, by the same sacrifices which are continually offered year after year, make perfect those who draw near. [2]Otherwise, would they not have ceased to be offered? If the worshipers had once been cleansed, they would no longer have any consciousness of sin. [3]But in these sacrifices there is a reminder of sin year after year. [4]For it is impossible that the blood of bulls and goats should take away sins.

Some questions to think about:

Is it ever possible to live completely according to the Law?	
How do we know, according to Hebrews, that the sacrifices under the Law never made sinners clean of sin?	
If the sinners could not be made clean by their sacrifices, then what was the purpose of those sacrifices?	

All these sacrifices had to be offered by priests from the tribe of Levi, which alone could produce men qualified to be priests. In return for their service, the tribe of Levi were in a sense relieved of more worldly cares. The other tribes were each assigned particular regions of Canaan to conquer and defend, but the Levites had no particular region of their own. Instead, they had a number of cities that belonged to them, giving them a steady income, and they were supported by the sacrifices of the people. That freedom from the everyday affairs of the conquest and administration of the Promised Land gave them the leisure they needed to devote themselves to their priestly service.

THE SACRIFICE OF THANKSGIVING

For a long time after the arrival in Canaan, Israel was a collection of bickering tribes constantly under threat from the powerful nations around them. But when David was accepted as king by all the tribes, a long period of peace and stability began. Israel grew into a small empire, whose power and prosperity drew people from all nations into its orbit.

The capital of this emerging empire was Jerusalem, which until David conquered it had belonged to an isolated Canaanite tribe. Once it was the capital of David's kingdom, he quickly moved to make it the center of worship for all Israel. His son Solomon would build the Temple there, which would become the one place on all the earth where the true worship of God could be celebrated.

2 Chronicles 6

³Then the king [Solomon] faced about, and blessed all the assembly of Israel, while all the assembly of Israel stood. ⁴And he said, "Blessed be the Lord, the God of Israel, who with his hand has fulfilled what he promised with his mouth to David my father, saying, ⁵"Since the day that I brought my people out of the land of Egypt, I chose no city in all the tribes of Israel in which to build a house, that my name might be there, and I chose no man as prince over my people Israel; ⁶but I have chosen Jerusalem that my name may be there and I have chosen David to be over my people Israel.'"

Jerusalem became the city where God's name would dwell. God chose that place for his Temple, and from then on until the end of the sacrificial cult, the Temple would be the center of sacrifices for the whole nation of Israel.

David had the usual business to deal with as king: wars, rebellions, trade, and so forth. But as much of his effort as he could spare was put into building up the liturgy of God's service in Jerusalem. And with David we see a new emphasis in that liturgy. Now we constantly hear about the "sacrifice of thanksgiving." We hear of it especially in the Psalms, and we remember that David himself wrote many of those hymns of the liturgy of Israel.

The Law made provisions for the sacrifice of thanksgiving (see Leviticus 7:12-16), but we don't hear anything about it until David's time. In 1 Chronicles, we read that David instituted regular thanksgiving liturgies in Jerusalem on the day he brought the Ark of the Covenant into the city — the Ark that held the stone tablets of the Law that Moses had brought down from Sinai:

1 CHRONICLES 16

¹And they brought the ark of God, and set it inside the tent which David had pitched for it; and they offered burnt offerings and peace offerings before God. ²And when David had finished offering the burnt offerings and the peace offerings, he blessed the people in the name of the LORD, ³and distributed to all Israel, both men and women, to each a loaf of bread, a portion of meat, and a cake of raisins.

⁴Moreover he appointed certain of the Levites as ministers before the ark of the LORD, to invoke, to thank, and to praise the LORD, the God of Israel.... ⁵Asaph was to sound the cymbals, ⁶and Benaiah and Jahaziel the priests were to blow trumpets continually, before the ark of the covenant of God.

⁷Then on that day David first appointed that thanksgiving be sung to the LORD by Asaph and his brethren.

A few questions to help focus on the reading:

What did David distribute to the people after he had made the offerings prescribed in the Law?	
What were the duties of the Levites who were assigned to minister before the Ark?	
What kind of occasion do we think of when we hear trumpets blowing?	

David was a famous musician and the great hymn-writer of ancient Israel, and many of the hymns in the book of Psalms are attributed to him. The Psalms are where we encounter the "sacrifice of thanksgiving" over and over. In Psalm 50, for example — a psalm attributed to Asaph, whom David left in charge of singing thanksgiving — we hear the voice of God, proclaiming that the sacrifice of thanksgiving is really more important than all those other sacrifices:

Psalm 50

12"If I were hungry, I would not tell you;
    for the world and all that is in it is mine.
13Do I eat the flesh of bulls,
    or drink the blood of goats?
14Offer to God a sacrifice of thanksgiving,
    and pay your vows to the Most High;
15and call upon me in the day of trouble;
    I will deliver you, and you shall glorify me."

Psalm 116 is heard in Christian liturgies all over the world:

PSALM 116

> [12]What shall I render to the LORD
>   for all his bounty to me?
> [13]I will lift up the cup of salvation
>   and call on the name of the LORD,
> [14]I will pay my vows to the LORD
>   in the presence of all his people. . . .
> [17]I will offer to you the sacrifice of thanksgiving
>   and call on the name of the LORD.
> [18]I will pay my vows to the LORD
>   in the presence of all his people,
> [19]in the courts of the house of the LORD,
>   in your midst, O Jerusalem.
> Praise the LORD!

In many Greek writers, this "sacrifice of thanksgiving" — *todah* in Hebrew — is translated *eucharistia* (yoo-ka-ris-TEE-uh), which is the word from which we get "Eucharist." It was a word the early Christians would have known very well.

Now we can look at some of the details of the readings we've just seen in a new light.

When David brought the Ark into Jerusalem, he distributed bread and raisins — dried grapes — to the people. The people all shared in the *eucharistia* by sharing David's bread and grapes.

In Psalm 116, the psalmist "will lift up the cup of salvation" — a "cup" we hear of in the context of the *eucharistia*. When Christians celebrate the Eucharist, of course, we celebrate with bread and wine — the cup of salvation is the cup of Christ's blood.

THE LITURGY OF THE TEMPLE

David established the liturgy and made plans for the building, but it was left to his son Solomon to build the Temple.

He chose a location with remarkably holy associations. We remember that Abraham was directed to offer Isaac as a sacrifice on the mountains of Moriah. Tradition says that the very hill on which Abraham prepared to sacrifice Isaac was the hill on which Solomon built his Temple.

This sacrifice of thanksgiving becomes the characteristic Temple liturgy in the kingdom of Israel, and later of Judah, the remnant left to David's descendants after the northern tribes rebelled and set up their own kingdom. The priests of the Temple were kept busy celebrating God's bounty in song and sacrifice.

How do we get from there — the Temple liturgy of God's chosen people, presided over by men from only one particular tribe — to the Christian Church, which makes no distinctions at all between tribes and nations?

The prophets foretold a time when the wall that separated Israelites from Gentiles (all the other nations of the world) would come down, and even eunuchs — who under the Law could have no part in the congregation (Deuteronomy 23:1) — would be welcome in the Temple of God:

Isaiah 56

³Let not the foreigner who has joined himself to the LORD say,
    "The LORD will surely separate me from his people";
and let not the eunuch say
    "Behold, I am a dry tree."
⁴For thus says the LORD:
    "To the eunuchs who keep my sabbaths,
who choose the things that please me
    and hold fast my covenant,
⁵I will give in my house and within my walls
    a monument and a name
    better than sons and daughters;
I will give them an everlasting name
    which shall not be cut off.

⁶And the foreigners who join themselves to the LORD,
    to minister to him, to love the name of the LORD,
    and to be his servants,
every one who keeps the sabbath, and does not profane it,
    and holds fast my covenant —
⁷these I will bring to my holy mountain,
    and make them joyful in my house of prayer;
their burnt offerings and their sacrifices
    will be accepted on my altar;
for my house shall be called a house of prayer for all peoples."

Some questions to think about:

What are the conditions under which foreigners and eunuchs are brought to the holy mountain?	
Who today might be in the position of the eunuchs and foreigners — outsiders looking in and despairing of ever belonging to the Church?	
What can we do to give them "an everlasting name"?	

The time was coming. But when? And how? The Lord's own city, Jerusalem, was destroyed by the Babylonians, and the Temple with it. When a feeble remnant returned to the wreckage about seventy years later, they put up a Temple that was far from the glorious structure of Solomon's time — and they responded to Israel's history of apostasy by becoming less tolerant of foreigners rather than more welcoming.

It would take nothing less than a miracle to bring about what the prophets had foretold.

IN PRACTICE . . .

We talked about both sacrifices for sin and sacrifices of thanksgiving in this session. Let's examine our consciences, first of all, and ask a few probing questions:

- Have I consciously sinned against anyone I know?
- When I look back at the past few days, can I think of any occasions when I accidentally sinned — when I offended someone without meaning to, or forgot one of the obligations I'd taken on?
- What have I done to put right what I did wrong?

Now let's look at what's gone right:

- What are some of God's greatest benefits to me?
- What are the things I enjoy most in my life?

Let's spend some time thinking and praying about both lists: the list of things we did wrong, and the list of things God has done right for us. The next time we go to Mass, we can keep both lists in mind, and remember to join our particular prayers to the prayers of the whole Church.

Jesus, the Great High Priest

BEFORE YOU START . . .

Read Hebrews 4:14 to 5:10.

After you've read that section, look back at the reading and think about these questions. You can write down your answers here. Feel free to change them as you read on.

Why can Jesus "deal gently" with us when we sin?	
Who ultimately appoints a priest?	
How is Jesus like an ordinary human priest? How is he different?	

BY WHAT AUTHORITY?

We can see two important aspects of Christ's mission when we look at the Gospels: his *service* and his *authority*. Both are aspects of the priest's office, and they both come out of the priest's position as mediator between God and humanity.

The priest must serve his people, because God desires only the good of his people.

The priest must have authority to make his service effective. He represents God's authority to the people.

When Jesus began his ministry, his *authority* was one of the first things the traditional religious leaders noticed about him. "And they were astonished at his teaching, for he taught them as one who had authority, and not as the scribes" (Mark 1:22).

Jesus taught as though he had a right to proclaim the truth, not just to debate the opinions of eminent scholars as the scribes would do. Nor was it only over humans that he claimed authority. The demons acknowledged his authority before many of the people were willing to acknowledge it: "What is this?" the people asked when they saw him expel an unclean spirit. "A new teaching! With authority he commands even the unclean spirits, and they obey him."

Most disturbing of all to the powers in charge of religious affairs in Jerusalem, Jesus even claimed authority over the Temple itself. When he found the outer court of the Temple full of hawkers selling their wares, he threw down their tables and chased the vendors out. "Is it not written, 'My house shall be called a house of prayer for all the nations'?" he demanded. "But you have made it a den of robbers" (Mark 11:17).

Jesus' outburst of righteous anger is all the more significant when we realize that the vendors had filled up the Court of the Gentiles, the part of the Temple complex that was supposed to be open for people of all nations to come and worship the true God.

Mark tells us that, after the cleansing of the Temple, the chief priests and scribes "sought a way to destroy him" (Mark 11:18). Jesus was claiming authority over their domain. In effect, he was claiming to replace the chief priests, who were in charge of the Temple.

THE PERFECT PRIEST

Jesus was indeed replacing the chief priests, because he fulfilled the mission of the priest in a perfect way that they could never hope to imitate, even if they had been more concerned about the spiritual welfare of the people than about their own power and influence. He was both truly divine and truly human. No one else could mediate between God and humanity in the same way.

HEBREWS 2

[14]Since therefore the children share in flesh and blood, he himself likewise partook of the same nature, that through death he might destroy him who has the power of death, that is, the devil, [15]and deliver all those who through fear of death were subject to lifelong bondage. [16]For surely it is not with angels that he is concerned but with the descendants of Abraham. [17]Therefore he had to be made like his brethren in every respect, so that he might become a merciful and faithful high priest in the service of God, to make expiation for the sins of the people. [18]For because he himself has suffered and been tempted, he is able to help those who are tempted.

Some questions to help us look closely at the reading:

What, according to Hebrews, holds us captive all our lives if we don't have Christ?	
How does Christ take us out of that captivity?	

The whole Letter to the Hebrews is really a meditation on Christ's role as priest, and how he perfects the priesthood in a way that was never possible for the Levitical priesthood under the Law. In fact, Hebrews tells us, Christ is the fulfillment of that promise in the Psalms of a priest after the order of Melchizedek.

HEBREWS 7

[11]Now if perfection had been attainable through the Levitical priesthood (for under it the people received the law), what further need would there have been for another priest to arise after the order of Melchizedek, rather than one named after the order of Aaron? [12]For when there is a change in the priesthood, there is necessarily a change in the law as well. [13]For the one of whom these things are spoken belonged to another tribe, from which no one has ever served at the altar. [14]For it is evident that our Lord was descended from Judah, and in connection with that tribe Moses said nothing about priests.

[15]This becomes even more evident when another priest arises in the likeness of Melchizedek, [16]who has become a priest, not according to a legal requirement concerning bodily descent but by the power of an indestructible life. [17]For it is witnessed of him,

"You are a priest for ever,
    after the order of Melchizedek."

[18]On the one hand, a former commandment is set aside because of its weakness and uselessness [19](for the law made nothing perfect); on the other hand, a better hope is introduced, through which we draw near to God.

Some questions to help us look closely at the reading:

Could anyone ever follow the Law completely? Think of the Ten Commandments: how many of them have you broken in your life?	
Why is it important to point out what tribe Jesus came from ?	

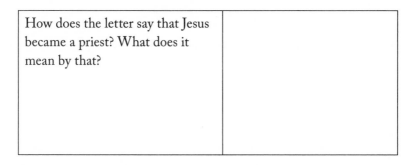

How does the letter say that Jesus became a priest? What does it mean by that?	

This is a very important argument. The sacrifices of the Old Testament, the letter says, could never take away sin. The priesthood of the Levites was *not good enough*. It was a necessary step on the way to our salvation, but it could never take away sin.

The very fact that Jesus did not come from the tribe of Levi is the evidence that he is a different kind of priest — the kind foreseen in Psalm 110:4: "You are a priest for ever, after the order of Melchizedek."

Since we know that the Law has no power to make us perfect, we have lost our hope in the Law. So we hope for a new kind of priest, a priest of a new law — a priest like that mysterious Melchizedek, who was priest of God Most High four hundred years before the Law was given to Israel.

That can give us a new hope. Melchizedek, who was a priest of the true God, blessed Abraham, and it was through Abraham that God's blessing would come to all the nations. What's important is that Melchizedek represents an older, more perfect priesthood, before Israel's sin made the Law necessary. Remember that the Levites were made the priestly tribe because of Israel's apostasy. Going back to the priesthood of Melchizedek is undoing that rebellion. Jesus the priest brings back the perfect obedience that Israel failed to exercise.

Now we can recall what Paul said about the Law: that "the law was our custodian until Christ came, that we might be justified by faith" (Galatians 3:24). It was never meant to be a permanent institution: it was meant to keep God's people on the right path, and to raise up Israel as a nation committed to holiness, until Christ came to supersede it with the perfect law.

THE HIGH PRIEST OF THE NEW LAW

When Moses brought the Law from God to the people, he led the people in a covenant ceremony that was meant to seal their submission to everything God had told them:

EXODUS 24

³Moses came and told the people all the words of the LORD and all the ordinances; and all the people answered with one voice, and said, "All the words which the LORD has spoken we will do." ⁴And Moses wrote all the words of the LORD. And he rose early in the morning, and built an altar at the foot of the mountain, and twelve pillars, according to the twelve tribes of Israel. ⁵And he sent young men of the people of Israel, who offered burnt offerings and sacrificed peace offerings of oxen to the LORD. ⁶And Moses took half of the blood and put it in basins, and half of the blood he threw against the altar. ⁷Then he took the book of the covenant, and read it in the hearing of the people; and they said, "All that the LORD has spoken we will do, and we will be obedient." ⁸And Moses took the blood and threw it upon the people, and said, "Behold the blood of the covenant which the LORD has made with you in accordance with all these words."

This is a kind of sacramental liturgy, in which the ceremony of sprinkling the blood half on the people and half on the altar — which represents the presence of God — binds the people to God, and to their promise to do everything the Lord has told them to do. By that liturgy, they bound themselves to the Law. We could say that the people are brought into communion with God through the blood of the sacrifice.

Jesus Christ was very much aware that he was bringing a new law, one that would fulfill the intention of the old Law of Moses — to make us a holy nation of priests — in a perfect way. His new law required a sacramental liturgy that would show how it perfected and superseded the Law of Moses and the sacrifices of the Old Testament.

MATTHEW 26

²⁶Now as they were eating, Jesus took bread, and blessed, and broke it, and gave it to the disciples and said, "Take, eat; this is my body."

²⁷And he took a cup, and when he had given thanks he gave it to them, saying, "Drink of it, all of you; ²⁸for this is my blood of the covenant, which is poured out for many for the forgiveness of sins. ²⁹I tell you I shall not drink again of this fruit of the vine until that day when I drink it new with you in my Father's kingdom."

Some questions to help us look closely at the reading:

Where does Jesus use the same words as Moses?	
What does Jesus do just before he breaks the bread?	
What is the purpose of Jesus' blood's being spilled?	

We recognize this liturgy, of course: it's the Eucharist, as Jesus instituted it at the Last Supper. We hear those words every time we go to Mass, but how often do we stop to think how significant they are?

"This is my blood of the covenant" can only mean one thing. Jesus is telling the disciples that this is a moment as decisive in history as the moment when Israel accepted the burden of the Law in the time of Moses. By drinking from the cup, the apostles are binding themselves to the new law that Jesus has been teaching them for three years now.

All the accounts of the Last Supper also tell us that Jesus "gave thanks." Remember that the *eucharistia*, the thanksgiving, had become the most important liturgy in Jerusalem since David's time. In effect, the Last Supper transfers the sacrificial ministry of the Temple to the new generation of Christian priests who will follow Jesus' new law.

This is the beginning of Jesus' sacrifice, the perfect sacrifice that reaches its completion on the Cross, where Jesus becomes both priest and sacrifice, offering himself as a sacrifice for our sins.

But who are the priests of this new law? The surprising answer, as we'll see in the next session, is that *we all are.*

When Jesus died, the curtain of the Temple was torn from top to bottom (Matthew 27:51). That curtain was what separated the rest of the Temple from the Holy of Holies, where only the high priest could enter. That separation was ripped away by the sacrifice of Jesus Christ on the Cross. The basic distinction between priest and people had been eliminated.

IN PRACTICE...

We talked a little about the *service* and the *authority* of Jesus' priesthood. The service can work for us only if we submit to the authority. Let's look into our own lives for a while:

- Where are we still fighting against Christ's authority?
- How can we train ourselves to submit to Christ, even in those areas where we resist?
- Where would we go for help? Whom could we ask for advice?
- What might we gain from submitting to the will of Christ, even where we stubbornly resist?

For the next few days, let's think about these questions and carefully try to pierce through the wall of self-deception we build up around ourselves when we don't want to do what God wants us to do.

We the Priests

BEFORE YOU START . . .

Read 1 Corinthians, chapters 12 and 13.

After you've read those two chapters, look back at the reading and think about these questions. You can write down your answers here. Feel free to change them as you read on.

How do we distinguish whether a calling comes from the Spirit or not?	
If everyone is part of the same body, why does Paul list offices according to rank (12:28)?	
What does Paul mean when he says to "earnestly desire the higher gifts" (12:31)? Should we be dissatisfied with our current jobs?	
What does "love" have to do with your own daily work?	

ONE VOCATION, MANY VOCATIONS

When people talk about "vocations," they're often talking about the priesthood and religious life (the life of monks and nuns, sisters and brothers). But priesthood and religious life are not the only vocations. Every one of us has a vocation.

We need to remember that we were created in the image of God. Merely being human is a great and noble calling, because God made us to be like him. As humans, made in God's image, we are called to *beatitude* — to blessedness and a share in God's kingdom. We also have the Godlike attribute of *free will*, which means that we can choose to respond to that calling, or to ignore it.

Plumbers, accountants, farmers, lawyers, cashiers, taxi drivers — we are called to many different jobs, but in those jobs we all have the same calling. We are all called to be priests.

WE ARE PRIESTS

As soon as we were baptized, we became priests of God. We don't think about that very much, but we ought to think about it every day, every hour, every minute. Everything we do ought to be in the service of God, and everywhere we go we ought to remember that *we are priests*.

We're so used to thinking of "priests" as the men who wear the collar that it almost shocks us to hear that we, too, are priests. But that's a doctrine straight from Scripture. St. Peter himself, the first pope, calls us all to the priesthood in his first letter:

1 PETER 2

[4]Come to him, to that living stone, rejected by men but in God's sight chosen and precious; [5]and like living stones be yourselves built into a spiritual house, to be a holy priesthood, to offer spiritual sacrifices acceptable to God through Jesus Christ. [6]For it stands in Scripture:

> "Behold, I am laying in Zion a stone,
>   a cornerstone chosen and precious,
> and he who believes in him will not be put to shame."

[7]To you therefore who believe, he is precious, but for those who do not believe,

> "The very stone which the builders rejected
>> has become the head of the corner,"

[8]and

> "A stone that will make men stumble,
>> a rock that will make them fall";

for they stumble because they disobey the word, as they were destined to do.

[9]But you are a chosen race, a royal priesthood, a holy nation, God's own people, that you may declare the wonderful deeds of him who called you out of darkness into his marvelous light. [10]Once you were no people but now you are God's people; once you had not received mercy but now you have received mercy.

Some questions to think about:

Why does Peter say we were "no people"? What are we without Christ?	
If we are living stones to be built into a spiritual house, what does that mean for the way we relate to one another?	
What does Peter say are our duties as a royal priesthood?	

Look closely at those words "a chosen race, a royal priesthood." Those words describe exactly the mission given to the nation of Israel at Sinai. We've looked at this passage before:

EXODUS 19

⁴"You have seen what I did to the Egyptians, and how I bore you on eagles' wings and brought you to myself. ⁵Now therefore, if you will obey my voice and keep my covenant, you shall be my own possession among all peoples; for all the earth is mine, ⁶and you shall be to me a kingdom of priests and a holy nation."

Israel would fail in that mission, falling prey to the temptation to have all the nice things every other nation had — riches, and kings, and idols. But Abraham's descendants were still fulfilling their role in God's plan of salvation, preparing the way for all nations to be brought back to God through Jesus Christ.

Now that Christ has come, the very meaning of the words "chosen race" is turned inside out. Instead of being chosen because we belong to a particular race, we belong to the race of God's people because we are chosen.

Peter had already seen Jews, Greeks, Romans, Ethiopians, and people from all over the known world brought into the Church. When he used the word "race," he knew he was using it in a way that was completely different from the way we normally use it. This "race" he's talking about is not bound together by physical characteristics or language or culture. What binds us together is that we belong to God.

In fact, we're back to the priesthood of the Patriarchs — of Abraham, Isaac, and Jacob. Like them, we have a direct relationship with God. But this time, the patriarchal priesthood is perfected through Jesus Christ.

OUR PRIESTLY VOCATION

So, in a sense, we all have the same vocation. We are all called to be holy, and we are all called to be priests of God. More than that, we are all called to be apostles. Our mission is the mission Jesus Christ gave to his disciples: to go into all the world and make disciples of all nations.

But we do have many different ways of living that vocation. Some of us will be celibate priests who wear collars, which is a great and noble vocation. Some of us will be garbage collectors, and that is another great and noble vocation.

Living a moral life is itself an act of worship. We glorify God when we live according to Christ's teaching, putting ourselves forward as examples of Christian living, and drawing others to the truth by our example.

Wherever you do your daily work, there is your altar. There is where you offer sacrifice to God Most High. Your altar may be an assembly line, or a computer keyboard, or the strings of a violin, or a manure pile in a barn. Wherever you work, you can offer that work as a sacrifice to God. Even St. Paul, who counseled Christians to take good care of their ministers, worked as a tentmaker so that no one could accuse him of getting a free ride (see Acts 18:2-3).

When we come together for Mass, all our sacrifices are bound together in the Eucharist. The one perfect sacrifice that Christ offers on the Cross sweeps up all our individual sacrifices and carries them to heaven.

And because our sacrifices are joined with the perfect sacrifice of Christ on the Cross, the sacrifices we make every day are themselves, in a way, Eucharistic. They're part of that eternal perfect sacrifice.

Whatever our vocation, we find the complete fulfillment of it only in the Church, bringing our labors together with the labors of every other Christian.

In the Church, we receive the sacraments, which give us the strength to go out into the world and live our vocations the way we were meant to live them — as apostles, spreading the light of the Gospel throughout the world.

Baptism and Confirmation are the sacraments that make us part of the "nation of priests" that celebrates Christ's liturgy all over the world. We call that the *common priesthood of the faithful* — the priesthood we share with every believer.

With no distinction, every single Christian is called to serve as a priest in this way. Holy Orders, on the other hand, is the sacrament by which some men are particularly marked for God's service. Our ordained ministers — the men we call deacons, priests, and bishops — bring all our priestly service together in the liturgy of the universal Church.

Because we know Christ — or, rather, because Christ knows us — we can offer spiritual sacrifices as God's priests on earth. We'll continue that mission in heaven, when we'll see everything clearly that we can only see in hints and metaphors right now.

PRIESTS IN THE KINGDOM OF HEAVEN

We wait eagerly for the kingdom of heaven, and the last book of the Bible gives us a few veiled pictures of that kingdom.

Revelation begins with a greeting that establishes all of us, the Christian believers, as priests of God.

Revelation 1

[5]To him who loves us and has freed us from our sins by his blood [6]and made us a kingdom, priests to his God and Father, to him be glory and dominion for ever and ever. Amen.

Right away, we know that this book is about how we make up a kingdom of priests — fulfilling the mission that was given to Israel at Sinai. Unlike the old Levitical priesthood, this one is open to every believer from every nation.

Revelation 5

[8]And when he had taken the scroll, the four living creatures and the twenty-four elders fell down before the Lamb, each holding a harp, and with golden bowls full of incense, which are the prayers of the saints; [9]and they sang a new song, saying,

> "Worthy are you to take the scroll and to open its seals,
> for you were slain and by your blood
>   you ransomed men for God
> from every tribe and tongue and people and nation,
> [10]and have made them a kingdom and priests to our God,
> and they shall reign on earth."

We shall reign on earth: Christ has given us dominion over the fish of the sea, and over the birds of the air, and over every living thing that moves upon the earth. The priestly mission of Adam and Eve (see Genesis 1:28) is restored to us.

Revelation is sometimes hard to understand, because it's trying to describe things that are beyond mortal comprehension. But what Revelation makes clear is that the kingdom of heaven is already with us. We won't understand everything about it until we reach heaven ourselves, but every time we participate in the Mass, we're actually standing in a little corner of heaven. Our liturgy in our Christian churches is part of the great heavenly liturgy that goes on forever before the throne of God.

Some questions to think about:

How can we say we're standing in heaven at Mass, even when there are babies crying, and people coughing, and a choir that can't carry a tune in a bucket?	
Why is there liturgy in heaven?	
How does knowing that our earthly liturgy is a small part of the eternal heavenly liturgy change the way we think about it? How does it change the way we feel about going to Mass?	

DIFFERENT GIFTS, SAME SPIRIT

Just as we have different roles in daily life, we also have different parts to play in the Church. The Church needs all kinds of abilities, as St. Paul tells us:

1 CORINTHIANS 12

[4]Now there are varieties of gifts, but the same Spirit; [5]and there are varieties of service, but the same Lord; [6]and there are varieties of working, but it is the same God who inspires them all in every one. [7]To each is given the manifestation of the Spirit for the common good. [8]To one is given through the Spirit the utterance of wisdom, and to another the utterance of knowledge according to the same Spirit, [9]to another faith by the same Spirit, to another gifts of healing by the one Spirit, [10]to another the working of miracles, to another prophecy, to another the ability to distinguish between spirits, to another various kinds of tongues, to another the interpretation of tongues. [11]All these are inspired by one and the same Spirit, who apportions to each one individually as he wills.

Some questions to think about:

Where do you see yourself in Paul's list of spiritual gifts in the Church?	
According to Paul, who ultimately decides what your role in the Church should be?	

Everyone has a spiritual gift to share with the congregation — even if it's just a quiet faith that puts you in the same pew day after day or week after week. When we speak of the Church as the "body of Christ," we're using a striking metaphor that comes straight from Paul.

1 CORINTHIANS 12

[12]For just as the body is one and has many members, and all the members of the body, though many, are one body, so it is with Christ.

[13]For by one Spirit we were all baptized into one body — Jews or Greeks, slaves or free — and all were made to drink of one Spirit.

[14]For the body does not consist of one member but of many. [15]If the foot should say, "Because I am not a hand, I do not belong to the body," that would not make it any less a part of the body. [16]And if the ear should say, "Because I am not an eye, I do not belong to the body," that would not make it any less a part of the body. [17]If the whole body were an eye, where would be the hearing? If the whole body were an ear, where would be the sense of smell?

In the Church, we all have different vocations. But like the human body, the body of Christ needs all those different parts doing their different things. Only a few of us will be deacons, priests, nuns, or monks; many more will be carpenters or accountants. We are all called to a holy life, but not all of us are called to a specifically religious life.

Nevertheless, some of us are called to a religious life, and it's more important than ever that we encourage those people to answer that call.

DISCERNING VOCATIONS

As we'll see when we look at the apostles, Christ calls his ministers to him. Their job is to answer the call when they hear it.

But how do you know when you're hearing the call? Answering that question is what we call "discerning" a vocation. Everyone's path is a little different, but there are some things you can do to find your way along that path.

Pray. First of all, if you have any suspicion that you might have a vocation, you should be talking to God about it. Pray constantly.

Find out more. Do your research — maybe visit a convent or a monastery if you think you might be called in that direction.

Talk to someone. Ask people you trust to help you think it through: parents, priests in your parish, teachers or professors you know well. As you go further, you'll want to get advice from someone trained in helping people discern vocations, and your priest can help you find that advice.

Don't neglect the sacraments. Go to confession and receive the Eucharist regularly.

Trust God to make the right decision for you. As Pope Benedict XVI once said: "Do not be afraid of Christ. He takes nothing away, and he gives you everything."

Here are some questions for the rest of us to think about:

How can I help increase the number of people who answer Christ's call to the priesthood or a religious life?	
If someone I knew asked me how to know whether he had a vocation, what would I say?	

IN PRACTICE . . .

Remembering that we're all called to be priests gives us a different way of looking at the world. How do we see our jobs, our families, even our hobbies differently if we think about them as ways of offering sacrifice to God? Here are some questions we can ask ourselves:

- When I'm at work, how do other people see me?
- Does my work show that I take my vocation seriously?
- Even when I hate my job, am I doing my best for the people around me?
- At home, what lessons does my family learn from my example?
- Do my hobbies and recreational interests lead me — and the people who observe me — toward or away from God?

Think about these questions as honestly as possible, then try to write down *one thing* you can do at work, and *one thing* you can do at home, to bring you closer to fulfilling your priestly calling.

The Priesthood of the Apostles

BEFORE YOU START . . .

Read John, chapter 17.

After you've read that chapter, look back at the reading and think about these questions. You can write down your answers here. Feel free to change them as you read on.

How do you think Jesus is "glorified" in the apostles (verse 10)?	
We know how many mistakes the apostles made, and how often they stumbled along the way. What does Jesus mean when he says "they are not of this world"?	
How do the others for whom Jesus prays come to believe in him (verse 20)?	

PRIESTLY POWER

It's obvious that the power to found a church didn't come from the apostles themselves. We might almost suspect that Jesus chose these men deliberately to prove that the Church was no human institution.

The leader, Peter, was notoriously impetuous and prone to complete misunderstanding. More than that, he had denied Christ three times when Jesus was under arrest. The others were scarcely more impressive, bickering about who was most important even at the Last Supper.

No, the power to exercise their priestly functions came, not from the apostles, but from Christ himself. When he breathed on them and ordained them as leaders of his Church, he gave them the power they would need to conquer the world.

JOHN 20

[21]Jesus said to them again, "Peace be with you. As the Father has sent me, even so I send you." [22]And when he had said this, he breathed on them, and said to them, "Receive the Holy Spirit. [23]If you forgive the sins of any, they are forgiven; if you retain the sins of any, they are retained."

Remember the definition of a priest we took from Hebrews 5:1: "For every high priest chosen from among men is appointed to act on behalf of men in relation to God, to offer gifts and sacrifices for sins."

What Jesus is giving the disciples is a priestly power: he assigns them to deal with the sins of the people. It's more than a priestly power, in

---

The ministerial or hierarchical priesthood of bishops and priests, and the common priesthood of all the faithful participate, "each in its own proper way, in the one priesthood of Christ." While being "ordered one to another," they differ essentially. In what sense? While the common priesthood of the faithful is exercised by the unfolding of baptismal grace — a life of faith, hope, and charity, a life according to the Spirit —, the ministerial priesthood is at the service of the common priesthood. It is directed at the unfolding of the baptismal grace of all Christians. The ministerial priesthood is a *means* by which Christ unceasingly builds up and leads his Church. For this reason it is transmitted by its own sacrament, the sacrament of Holy Orders.

— *Catechism of the Catholic Church*, no. 1547

fact: he is giving them the decisive power to forgive or retain sins — the power he claimed that caused the Pharisees to accuse him of blasphemy.

But who were these men to whom Jesus gave this awesome power? How did they get to that position?

CALLING THE APOSTLES

Jesus knew he would not stay with us in bodily form forever. Knowing that he would go back to the Father, he made sure that his kingdom on earth was left with a structure that would keep it going until the end of time.

He didn't wait until his time was nearly up, either. Starting at the beginning of his ministry, he called twelve men to work closely with him in everything he did. They would watch and learn from his example; he would teach them the difficult truths about his kingdom.

MARK 1

[16]And passing along by the Sea of Galilee, he saw Simon and Andrew the brother of Simon casting a net in the sea; for they were fishermen. [17]And Jesus said to them, "Follow me and I will make you become fishers of men." [18]And immediately they left their nets and followed him. [19]And going on a little farther, he saw James the son of Zebedee and John his brother, who were in their boat mending the nets. [20]And immediately he called them; and they left their father Zebedee in the boat with the hired servants, and followed him.

This is the way Christ chooses his ministers: he calls, they answer. All the stories of Jesus calling various disciples are like that. Jesus approaches a man who's going about his daily business and says "Follow me," and the man follows.

The Gospels are almost frustratingly vague on what the disciples' reactions were. All we hear is that Jesus called, and they followed.

Some questions to think about:

Imagine yourself in the place of one of the disciples. What would it take to make you drop your job and follow a wandering preacher? What would you have to believe about the man you were following?	
Why do you think Mark's account doesn't tell us anything about what the apostles felt?	

Even St. Paul, who was called after Jesus ascended into heaven, follows the same pattern. He was off to Damascus to persecute some Christians when Jesus appeared and called to him.

ACTS 9

[3]Now as he journeyed he approached Damascus, and suddenly a light from heaven flashed about him. [4]And he fell to the ground and heard a voice saying to him, "Saul, Saul, why do you persecute me?" [5]And he said, "Who are you, Lord?" And he said, "I am Jesus, whom you are persecuting; [6]but rise and enter the city, and you will be told what you are to do."

Christ knew that he was leaving his Church in the hands of men who were, by worldly standards, ill-equipped for administering a large institution. At the Last Supper, Jesus prayed to the Father to strengthen the apostles:

JOHN 17

[14]I have given them your word; and the world has hated them because they are not of the world, even as I am not of the world. [15]I do not pray that you should take them out of the world, but

that you should keep them from the evil one. [16]They are not of the world, even as I am not of the world. [17]Sanctify them in the truth; your word is truth. [18]As you sent me into the world, so I have sent them into the world. [19]And for their sake I consecrate myself, that they also may be consecrated in truth.

[20]"I do not pray for these only, but also for those who believe in me through their word, [21]that they may all be one; even as you, Father, are in me, and I in you, that they also may be in us, so that the world may believe that you have sent me."

After the Resurrection, Jesus gave the apostles their mission — nothing less than to spread the Good News through the whole earth.

MATTHEW 28

[18]And Jesus came and said to them, "All authority in heaven and on earth has been given to me. [19]Go therefore and make disciples of all nations, baptizing them in the name of the Father and of the Son and of the Holy Spirit, [20]teaching them to observe all that I have commanded you; and lo, I am with you always, to the close of the age."

Notice that Jesus promises to be with them always, and notice that he ordains them to act as priests. Their job is to perform the sacrament of baptism wherever they go.

But Jesus did not send them out into the world with no preparation. After he rose from the dead, he spent some time preparing them for the duties they would have to assume when he was gone:

ACTS 1

[3]To them he presented himself alive after his passion by many proofs, appearing to them during forty days, and speaking of the kingdom of God. [4]And while staying with them he charged them not to depart from Jerusalem, but to wait for the promise of the Father, which, he said, "you heard from me, [5]for John baptized with water, but before many days you shall be baptized with the Holy Spirit."

[6]So when they had come together, they asked him, "Lord, will you at this time restore the kingdom to Israel?" [7]He said to them,

"It is not for you to know times or seasons which the Father has fixed by his own authority. [8]But you shall receive power when the Holy Spirit has come upon you; and you shall be my witnesses in Jerusalem and in all Judea and Samaria and to the end of the earth." [9]And when he had said this, as they were looking on, he was lifted up, and a cloud took him out of their sight.

A few questions to help us think about the reading:

How long did Jesus spend with the apostles after his Resurrection?	
What other things can you think of in the Bible that took place over the same number of days?	
What do the apostles have to wait for before they leave Jerusalem?	

ESTABLISHING THE SUCCESSION

The first thing the apostles did was to choose someone to replace Judas, who had killed himself after betraying Jesus. We can learn a lot about how the earliest Church worked just from this passage:

Acts 1

[15]In those days Peter stood up among the brethren (the company of persons was in all about a hundred and twenty), and said, [16]"Brethren, the scripture had to be fulfilled, which the Holy Spirit spoke beforehand by the mouth of David, concerning Judas who was guide to those who arrested Jesus. [17]For he was numbered among us, and was allotted his share in this ministry....

[20]For it is written in the book of Psalms,

> 'Let his habitation become desolate,
>> and let there be no one to live in it';

and

> 'His office let another take.'

[21]So one of the men who have accompanied us during all the time that the Lord Jesus went in and out among us, [22]beginning from the baptism of John until the day when he was taken up from us — one of these men must become with us a witness to his resurrection." [23]And they put forward two, Joseph called Barsabbas, who was surnamed Justus, and Matthias. [24]And they prayed and said, "Lord, who know the hearts of all men, show which one of these two you have chosen [25]to take the place in this ministry and apostleship from which Judas turned aside, to go to his own place." [26]And they cast lots for them, and the lot fell on Matthias; and he was enrolled with the eleven apostles.

Some questions to think about:

Why did the apostles need to find a successor to replace Judas Iscariot?	

Who led the apostles in making that decision?	
What qualifications did the apostles look for in someone to replace Judas?	

This incident shows us quite a bit about the structure of the Church Christ left behind on earth.

First, we can see that the apostles had accepted the idea of succession. The Church was going to last for an indefinite time, and the original Twelve would die. One of them was already dead. They would have to come up with a way of choosing successors, so that the Church continued when the apostles themselves were all gone.

Second, we can see Peter acting as the accepted leader. No one questions his authority to make this decision.

On the other hand, the apostles act in a body. Peter leads, but they follow with complete assent.

THE POWER OF THE HOLY SPIRIT

Jesus had instructed his apostles to wait in Jerusalem for the coming of the Holy Spirit. When the Spirit did come, all the power Jesus had promised the apostles came to them:

ACTS 2

[1]When the day of Pentecost had come, they were all together in one place. [2]And suddenly a sound came from heaven like the rush

of a mighty wind, and it filled all the house where they were sitting. ³And there appeared to them tongues as of fire, distributed and resting on each one of them. ⁴And they were all filled with the Holy Spirit and began to speak in other tongues, as the Spirit gave them utterance.

This power belongs to all the apostles of Christ, including Paul, even though he was called later — as "one untimely born" (1 Corinthians 15:8). Paul explicitly calls his apostolic office "priestly" when he writes to the Romans:

ROMANS 15

¹⁵But on some points I have written to you very boldly by way of reminder, because of the grace given me by God ¹⁶to be a minister of Christ Jesus to the Gentiles in the priestly service of the gospel of God, so that the offering of the Gentiles may be acceptable, sanctified by the Holy Spirit.

Paul came from the tribe of Benjamin, not Levi, so according to his old outlook — he used to be a Pharisee, after all — he had no business calling himself a priest. But the kingdom of Christ has swept away the old order. Or, rather, it has restored an even older order — the order of Melchizedek, when the distinctions of tribe and nation made no difference in the service of God.

Through the power of the Holy Spirit, the apostles were able to perform the same kinds of miracles Christ had performed when he was with them. But they were always careful to give the credit to Jesus.

SERVICE AND AUTHORITY

We have far more writing by Paul than by any other author in the New Testament, so a great deal of what we know about the administration of the early Church comes from what Paul wrote. And in those writings we can see that the mission of the apostles did indeed continue Jesus' mission in its two characteristic forms: service and authority. As with Jesus, the authority was only for the sake of the service.

We know that Paul worked tirelessly, traveling almost constantly when he wasn't in prison, laboring to build up and encourage the congregations he had planted. He was willing to do anything for Christ and for his brothers and sisters in Christ — even to giving up his own life, which he finally did in Rome.

But sometimes Paul found it necessary to remind his brothers and sisters of the authority Christ had given him. "What do you wish?" he once asked the church in Corinth (1 Corinthians 4:21). "Shall I come to you with a rod, or with love in a spirit of gentleness?"

He much preferred the spirit of gentleness, but he was willing to get out the rod if he had to.

But the authority was not for the purpose of building up Paul's power; it was only for building up the Church, and for steering the congregations he had planted in the right direction. In the case of Corinth, the church there was troubled by constant disagreements, and in the turbulent atmosphere people were forgetting the fundamental principles of Christian morality. To get the people back on track was Paul's mission; if that meant an unpleasant confrontation, he was ready for it, though he would rather avoid it. It was worth the price of a bit of unpleasantness if he could get a few souls back on their way to salvation.

Some questions to think about:

How do the priests in our own churches exercise the authority Christ gave them in order to build up the Church?	
Let's be honest: do we always respond well to that authority? Or are we sometimes more like the Corinthians in Paul's time, refusing to be led by the authority that tries to serve us?	

How can we teach ourselves to be properly submissive to legitimate authority in the Church?	

TAKING THE SACRAMENTS SERIOUSLY

The life of the early Church, like the life of our Church today, revolved around the Sacraments. The apostles devoted much of their time to the Eucharist. The very first thing we hear about the Church after the apostles received the Holy Spirit at Pentecost is Luke's brief description of how they lived:

ACTS 2

[41]So those who received his word were baptized, and there were added that day about three thousand souls. [42]And they devoted themselves to the apostles' teaching and fellowship, to the breaking of bread and to the prayers.

Once the apostles had baptized them, new converts spent much of their lives at Mass. They didn't call it that, of course, but they were listening to the Word and participating in the Eucharist. Already the apostles were acting as priests of the New Covenant.

The importance of the sacraments is a constant theme in the New Testament, and especially in Paul's letters. The words used in the Eucharistic liturgies of Christian churches all over the world come from Paul's first letter to the Corinthians:

I CORINTHIANS II

[23]For I received from the Lord what I also delivered to you, that the Lord Jesus on the night when he was betrayed took bread, [24]and when he had given thanks, he broke it, and said, "This is my body which is for you. Do this in remembrance of me." [25]In the same way

also the cup, after supper, saying, "This cup is the new covenant in my blood. Do this, as often as you drink it, in remembrance of me." [26]For as often as you eat this bread and drink the cup, you proclaim the Lord's death until he comes.

This is not just a simple memorial, the way we might celebrate a wake for a departed friend. It's a sacrament, which means it has real power. In fact, the power is so real that it's a matter of life and death. Paul goes on:

1 CORINTHIANS 11

[27]Whoever, therefore, eats the bread or drinks the cup of the Lord in an unworthy manner will be guilty of profaning the body and blood of the Lord. [28]Let a man examine himself, and so eat of the bread and drink of the cup. [29]For any one who eats and drinks without discerning the body eats and drinks judgment upon himself. [30]That is why many of you are weak and ill, and some have died.

Think of it: people are *dying* because they receive the Eucharist in an unworthy manner! Real power is manifested every time the apostles break bread. St. John Chrysostom compares it to the sacrifice of Elijah on Mt. Carmel.

You probably remember the story (1 Kings 18:17-40): Elijah challenged the priests of Baal to a contest. They would prepare a sacrifice on an altar, and he would do the same. Then they would pray to Baal to send fire from heaven, and Elijah would pray to the Lord. Of course, the priests of Baal got nowhere with their prayers, but when Elijah prayed, fire came down and consumed not only the sacrifice but the altar as well.

The apostles, and their successors the bishops and priests, preside over a greater miracle at every Mass. Elijah called down fire from heaven; the priest calls down the Holy Spirit, and makes Christ truly present on the altar.

The apostles would not live forever, and the Church grew so quickly that even in their lifetimes it was already necessary to appoint many more leaders to help oversee its business.

ACTS 6

²And the twelve summoned the body of the disciples and said, "It is not right that we should give up preaching the word of God to serve tables. ³Therefore, brethren, pick out from among you seven men of good repute, full of the Spirit and of wisdom, whom we may appoint to this duty. ⁴But we will devote ourselves to prayer and to the ministry of the word." ⁵And what they said pleased the whole multitude, and they chose Stephen, a man full of faith and of the Holy Spirit, and Philip, and Prochorus, and Nicanor, and Timon, and Parmenas, and Nicolaus, a proselyte of Antioch. ⁶These they set before the apostles, and they prayed and laid their hands upon them.

Some questions to help us examine the reading:

What were the qualifications the apostles looked for in a helper?	
What did the apostles need more time for?	
How did the apostles prepare the seven recruits for their work in the Church?	

These first seven "deacons," or helpers, were not simply chosen and told to go out and get to work. Before they were given their assignments, they went through an *ordination*: the apostles laid their hands on them, giving them power and authority in the same way that Christ had given power and authority to the apostles.

When Paul was ready to begin his work as an apostle, the other apostles laid their hands on him (Acts 13:2-4). Paul, in turn, laid his hands on Timothy when Timothy was ready to begin his work preaching and teaching (2 Timothy 1:6).

As the years have gone on, and the Church has grown to more than a billion people, all her ministers have been ordained in that way, in an unbroken chain that goes straight back to Christ. The bishops and priests we know today are truly the successors to the apostles.

IN PRACTICE...

Many people — especially Protestants, but also some within the Catholic Church — assert that the structure of the Church, with its ordained priesthood, its levels of authority, and its strong emphasis on sacraments, is a medieval invention.

We've seen enough to know that the Church of the apostles already had a strong emphasis on sacraments, and that Christ and his apostles themselves instituted the basic structure of the Church. Here's your chance for a little research project:

- How would you respond to someone who thought the Church was a medieval invention?
- Where would you look in Scripture for your responses?
- How is the Church today like the Church of the apostles?
- How is it different, and do the differences matter?

Spending some time answering these questions will not only help you defend your faith against some of the most common attacks on it, but it might also lead you to a much deeper appreciation of the Church we know.

The Biblical Priesthood Today

BEFORE YOU START . . .

Read 1 Timothy, chapter 3.

After you've read that chapter, look back at the reading and think about these questions. You can write down your answers here. Feel free to change them as you read on.

Why do you think the work of a bishop is "a noble task"?	
Why is it so important that the bishop or deacon have a well-managed household of his own?	
We can see how the Church needs good ministers, but what do you think Paul sees as the benefit to the person who serves as deacon or bishop?	

We've seen what a vocation is like. You'll remember how Jesus chose his disciples:

MARK 1

[16]And passing along by the Sea of Galilee, he saw Simon and Andrew the brother of Simon casting a net in the sea; for they were fishermen. [17]And Jesus said to them, "Follow me and I will make you become fishers of men." [18]And immediately they left their nets and followed him. [19]And going on a little farther, he saw James the son of Zebedee and John his brother, who were in their boat mending the nets. [20]And immediately he called them; and they left their father Zebedee in the boat with the hired servants, and followed him.

The disciples did not call for Jesus; indeed, the Gospel stories seem to go out of their way to show that the disciples weren't even thinking about Jesus, or about matters of faith at all, when Jesus suddenly appeared and called them.

He still calls, and there are still people who answer his call. Of course, he calls every one of us to be a priest of God, to live a truly moral life, and to share eternal joy in heaven. But in a more particular way Jesus calls certain people to himself to serve his flock. The sacrament that marks these people as Christ's ministers is called *Holy Orders*. When a man has received Holy Orders, we say that he has been *ordained*.

WHO CAN BE ORDAINED?

No one can simply decide to be a priest; Christ must call him. This call is a *grace*, and like every grace of God, it comes to us not because we deserve it but because God chooses to give it to us.

If a man thinks he has been called by Christ, it's the Church's job to examine and decide whether this was truly a call from Christ. If so, the Church will call him to the priesthood and train him for the work.

Only men can be ordained in this way, and these days many people ask why that is. Men and women are equal in most jobs; women have been presidents and prime ministers of powerful nations. Does the Church believe that women are inferior?

Anyone who considers how the Church venerates the Blessed Virgin can hardly think the Church considers women inferior. To Mary

Magdalene went the honor of being the first to see the risen Christ, and tradition venerates her with the title "Apostle to the Apostles." Women have been powerful examples of faith throughout history.

But the Church is bound to follow the example of Christ, who chose twelve men to be his apostles. The apostles, in turn, chose men to succeed them, and so on down to our time. These successors to the apostles, the bishops, represent Christ to us. The priests, the bishops' colleagues and coworkers, stand as fathers to their flocks. It is not possible for the Church to ordain women.

St. Paul lays out what's required of a bishop in his first letter to Timothy, a leader in the early Church who had worked closely with Paul.

1 Timothy 3

[2]Now a bishop must be above reproach, the husband of one wife, temperate, sensible, dignified, hospitable, an apt teacher, [3]no drunkard, not violent but gentle, not quarrelsome, and no lover of money. [4]He must manage his own household well, keeping his children submissive and respectful in every way; [5]for if a man does not know how to manage his own household, how can he care for God's Church? [6]He must not be a recent convert, or he may be puffed up with conceit and fall into the condemnation of the devil; [7]moreover he must be well thought of by outsiders, or he may fall into reproach and the snare of the devil.

The main point of Paul's list is that the bishop needs to remember that his flock looks to him as the pattern of Christian life. Specifically, he must be

- The husband of one wife
- Temperate
- Sensible, dignified, and gentle
- A good teacher
- A good host
- A good manager in his own household

On the other hand, he must *not* be

- A drunkard

- A money-lover
- Violent or quarrelsome
- A new convert

And Paul has one last qualification that might surprise us, given what we know about the persecutions suffered by the early Christians: the bishop must always have a good reputation outside the Church.

Some questions to think about:

Why is it important that the bishop should not be a new convert?	
Why does Paul worry so much about the bishop's personal life? If he does his job well, shouldn't that be enough?	

CELIBACY

You may have noticed that celibacy is not one of Paul's requirements in the list of traits of a good bishop he gave to Timothy. Scripture does not require priests to be celibate, but merely of outstanding moral character.

We should remember, however, that celibacy has always been recommended as a good thing, though not required. When Jesus made his famous pronouncement prohibiting divorce, his disciples were a bit taken aback.

MATTHEW 19

[10]The disciples said to him, "If such is the case of a man with his wife, it is not expedient to marry." [11]But he said to them, "Not all men can receive this precept, but only those to whom it is given. [12]For there

are eunuchs who have been so from birth, and there are eunuchs who have been made eunuchs by men, and there are eunuchs who have made themselves eunuchs for the sake of the kingdom of heaven. He who is able to receive this, let him receive it."

"He who is able" to be celibate "for the sake of the kingdom of God" is doing a good thing.

Different rites of the Church observe different traditional disciplines for the priesthood. All of them are based on Paul's principles, but adapted to different environments.

In many Eastern churches, a married man may be ordained as a priest. He may not, however, marry after he has been ordained. If his wife dies, he remains a widower; if he was not married before, he remains celibate. Bishops in these Eastern churches are always celibate.

Although celibacy is the rule for priests in the Western or Latin-rite church, there are some exceptions. In America, there are Byzantine-rite churches serving the descendants of immigrants from eastern Europe, and in some of these churches the clergy are married. Some married Protestant ministers who have left their Protestant churches and come home to the Catholic Church have been accepted for ordination as Catholic priests.

These instances are rare exceptions, however. In the Western church, celibacy is the rule. But again, if celibacy isn't required by Scripture, why does the Latin-rite church require it? The answer is that, while Paul does not absolutely prescribe celibacy, he recommends it to anyone who wants to concentrate on divine things.

1 CORINTHIANS 7

[32]I want you to be free from anxieties. The unmarried man is anxious about the affairs of the Lord, how to please the Lord; [33]but the married man is anxious about worldly affairs, how to please his wife, [34]and his interests are divided. And the unmarried woman or virgin is anxious about the affairs of the Lord, how to be holy in body and spirit; but the married woman is anxious about worldly affairs, how to please her husband. [35]I say this for your own benefit,

not to lay any restraint upon you, but to promote good order and to secure your undivided devotion to the Lord.

Over the centuries, the Church has found — not surprisingly — that Paul gives good advice. Everyone has heard stories of the corruption in the Church during the Middle Ages and the Renaissance. One of the main reasons for that corruption was that some bishops had not taken their vows of celibacy seriously. They had families to look after, sons to place in good jobs. They were anxious about worldly affairs.

That bitter experience is one of the reasons why the Church in the West still takes the vow of celibacy so seriously.

It is also true that a priest must be a father to his flock, as we saw before. A good father sacrifices his own interest for his children, and a good priest sacrifices his own interest for his congregation.

There are many both inside and outside the Church who argue that priestly celibacy is an outdated notion. Some, seduced by pop psychology and pointing to recent scandals in the Church, even argue that celibacy is unhealthy, repressing the sex instinct so that it bursts out in some sort of explosion of perversion. (In fact, Roman Catholic priests are no more likely to be sex criminals than married clergy of other religious groups.)

Those arguments miss the point. Precisely because of the temptations of our sex-crazed society, priestly celibacy is all the more important today. Not only does it remove the distraction most characteristic of worldliness in our time, but it also shows the lust-ridden world an example of higher love.

Sex is a good thing; marriage is a sacrament, and sex is part of what makes marriage holy and turns two separate people into a family, an earthly mirror of the heavenly love of the Trinity.

But there is a higher world than this one, where marriage is unknown and unnecessary because everyone lives in perfect knowledge. A celibate priesthood is a constant reminder of that world, always pointing in the direction of heaven when the rest of the world is turning in on itself.

And the celibate life is a life of joy to those who sincerely apply themselves to it. Many priests learn to see it not as a restriction, but as a freedom from restrictions — "freedom for the ministry," as the late Fr. Richard John Neuhaus put it.

MARK 10

[29]Jesus said, "Truly, I say to you, there is no one who has left house or brothers or sisters or mother or father or children or lands, for my sake and for the gospel, [30]who will not receive a hundredfold now in this time, houses and brothers and sisters and mothers and children and lands, with persecutions, and in the age to come eternal life."

The celibate priest, or monk, or nun, has given up the prospect of a limited family for the prospect of an unlimited family — for making the whole world into brothers and sisters and children.

Some questions to think about:

Try to remember some conversations you've had about priestly celibacy with people who didn't like the idea. What were their arguments?	
How do you answer those arguments? What have those people misunderstood or overlooked?	
How should those of us who have been called to marriage take the celibate priesthood as our example? What lessons do we learn from it?	

A PRIEST FOREVER

Once he is ordained, a priest is a priest forever. Just as baptism marks us forever with the seal of Christ, Holy Orders gives a priest a sacred character, a likeness to Christ, that can never be erased.

That doesn't mean the priest can't abuse his position. Priests are men, sinners with free will. They can commit theft, adultery, murder, and every sin our depraved human minds can conceive. They can be stripped of their authority to celebrate the sacraments. But they are priests nonetheless; that indelible character never goes away.

So a priest is not a priest because he celebrates the sacraments, or because he wears the collar, or because of anything else he does. The actions don't make the priest; the sacrament does. A father is not a father because he changes diapers or helps with homework; he simply is the father of his children, whether he does anything for them or not. A priest is a priest, even if he dishonors his priesthood. He isn't a priest because he administers the sacraments; he administers the sacraments because he is a priest.

2 TIMOTHY 1

[6]For this reason I remind you to rekindle the gift of God that is within you through the laying on of my hands; [7]for God did not give us a spirit of timidity but a spirit of power and love and self-control.

As Paul says, the gift of God came through the *sacrament* — the laying on of hands. If Timothy is being too timid, that doesn't make him any less what he is. The "spirit of power and love and self-control" that came to him through the laying on of hands is still in him.

Some questions to think about:

We often hear stories in the news about priests who have gone wrong, perhaps because a priest doing his work well isn't news. How do the reports seem to misunderstand the character of the priesthood?	

How can we help our neighbors overcome their misunderstandings about the character of the priesthood?	
If the priest bears the likeness of Christ, how should that affect the way we relate to the priests we know?	

THE HIERARCHY

"Hierarchy" literally means the government of holy things. We use the word to describe the order of the government of the Church, from lay believers through deacons, priests, and bishops all the way up to the Holy Father.

It's probably obvious why we need some order in a group of a billion people. There must be some organization and authority, or no one will know who's supposed to be doing what.

But the hierarchy isn't necessarily like secular governments. Or, rather, we might say that secular governments have imitated the hierarchy of the Church.

When we think of a kingdom, like France under Louis XIV or Rome under the emperors, we think of one ruler at the top who has people to serve him, and they have people to serve them, and so on down the line, until we reach the ordinary peasant at the bottom of the chain, who is below everybody.

That's certainly the kind of kingdom Jesus' disciples were imagining. They imagined themselves as big men in his kingdom, with lots of underlings to tend to their every whim. The only question was which one of them was going to be the biggest of them all.

MARK 9

[33]And they came to Capernaum; and when he was in the house he asked them, "What were you discussing on the way?" [34]But they were silent; for on the way they had discussed with one another who was the greatest. [35]And he sat down and called the Twelve and he said to them, "If any one would be first, he must be last of all and servant of all." [36]And he took a child, and put him in the midst of them; and taking him in his arms, he said to them, [37]"Whoever receives one such child in my name receives me; and whoever receives me, receives not me but him who sent me."

This is a hard lesson for us to learn: the leaders are the servants of all. It's not at all how we imagine being a big man in the kingdom. Being somebody important is supposed to mean having people take care of you, not the other way around. Think about these questions:

Why were the disciples embarrassed about what they'd been discussing?	
Why would you want to be first if it means you have to be last?	
Why a child? What does the child have to do with the question the disciples were debating?	

This certainly was a hard lesson for the disciples to learn. They brought up the question again and again, and Jesus showed truly super-human patience with them. Even at the Last Supper, we find them arguing yet again about which one was the greatest.

LUKE 22

24A dispute also arose among them, which of them was to be regarded as the greatest. 25And he said to them, "The kings of the Gentiles exercise lordship over them; and those in authority over them are called benefactors. 26But not so with you; rather let the greatest among you become as the youngest, and the leader as one who serves. 27For which is the greater, one who sits at table, or one who serves? Is it not the one who sits at table? But I am among you as one who serves."

Here, Jesus uses his own example to illustrate the principle. The world thinks of the servant as being in the low position, and the person served as the great one. But Jesus lives as a servant. In John's Gospel, we read how he brought the point home with a striking demonstration. It's a long passage, but every detail is important:

JOHN 13

1Now before the feast of the Passover, when Jesus knew that his hour had come to depart out of this world to the Father, having loved his own who were in the world, he loved them to the end. 2And during supper, when the devil had already put it into the heart of Judas Iscariot, Simon's son, to betray him, 3Jesus, know-ing that the Father had given all things into his hands, and that he had come from God and was going to God, 4rose from supper, laid aside his garments, and girded himself with a towel. 5Then he poured water into a basin, and began to wash the disciples' feet, and to wipe them with the towel with which he was girded. 6He came to Simon Peter; and Peter said to him, "Lord, do you wash my feet?" 7Jesus answered him, "What I am doing you do not know now, but afterward you will understand." 8Peter said to him, "You shall never wash my feet." Jesus answered him, "If I do not wash you, you have no part in me." [9]Simon Peter said to him, "Lord, not my feet only but also my hands and my head!" [10]Jesus said to him, "He who has bathed does not need to wash, except for his feet, but he is clean all over; and you are clean, but not every one of you." [11]For he knew who was to betray him; that was why he said, "You are not all clean."

[12]When he had washed their feet, and taken his garments, and resumed his place, he said to them, "Do you know what I have done to you? [13]You call me Teacher and Lord; and you are right, for so I am. [14]If I then, your Lord and Teacher, have washed your feet, you also ought to wash one another's feet. [15]For I have given you an example, that you also should do as I have done to you. [16]Truly, truly, I say to you, a servant is not greater than his master; nor is he who is sent greater than he who sent him. [17]If you know these things, blessed are you if you do them."

Even today in the Middle East, the feet are considered vile and dirty, almost obscene. Many a Western diplomat has inadvertently offended his hosts by thoughtlessly showing the soles of his shoes.

Think about these questions:

Why do you think Peter refuses to have his feet washed at first?	
What does Jesus tell him that makes him change his mind?	
What is Jesus talking about when he says that "he who has bathed does not need to wash"?	

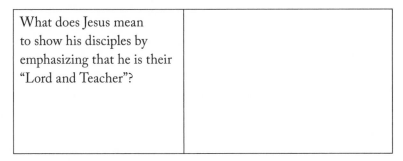

What does Jesus mean to show his disciples by emphasizing that he is their "Lord and Teacher"?	

Washing feet was not just a menial job, but a job that fell only to the lowest of servants. We can understand Peter's first reaction. It would hardly be more out of character if the Master had suddenly gone out to the stables and started to muck out the stalls!

But this is what a leader does in the Church. A Christian bishop is a prince, worthy of respect and attention. But he's worthy precisely because he stands ready to go into the stables with a pitchfork. His job is to serve all the priests in his diocese, so they can serve their parishes. And the Pope's job is to be the servant of the servants of God.

John gives us the whole key to this upside-down hierarchy right at the beginning of the story: love. "Having loved his own who were in the world, he loved them to the end." Jesus chose his disciples to be leaders in his Church, and he patiently taught them what that kind of leadership would mean. Even by the Last Supper, they were still thinking in earthly terms: glory, riches, honor, and ordering people around. But what Christian leadership really means is all right there in that image of Jesus kneeling with a towel wrapped around him, washing his disciples' filthy feet.

THE HIERARCHY TODAY

So what does this mean in the Christian life?

We are all priests of God; each one of us called to serve God in our own way. Whether we're collecting garbage or painting houses or managing accounts receivable, we do it as a service to God.

The ordained priesthood serves us by helping to guide our labors in the right direction, and by uniting us in the liturgy, so that every offering we make becomes part of the one eternal sacrifice of Christ on the Cross.

The so-called higher offices in the hierarchy serve the lower ones.

The bishops take care of coordinating the business of the diocese so that the deacons and priests can fulfill their service to the lay members; as teachers and leaders, the bishops make sure that the Christian liturgy and doctrine are transmitted, pure and unaltered, to every generation.

The Holy Father serves the bishops by making sure the doctrine of the Church is preserved down through the generations — so that the bishops know what they need to be teaching — and by steering the whole Church on the right course so the bishops can put things in the right order in their own areas.

LEVELS IN THE HIERARCHY

Fundamentally, there are three positions, or "degrees," in the ordained priesthood:

- Bishop
- Priest
- Deacon

Bishop. The word *bishop* comes from a Greek word meaning "supervisor" or "overseer." Bishops are successors to the apostles, consecrated by the laying on of hands in an unbroken line that goes straight back to Christ himself. (That unbroken line is called the *apostolic succession.*) The bishops receive the fullness of the Sacrament of Holy Orders, and they serve as the *high priests* of the Christian Church. Each bishop is responsible for a particular diocese, meaning all the congregations in a certain geographical area. Together, however, the bishops are responsible for the mission of the whole Church. Each bishop, like the twelve apostles before him, is the personal representative of Christ, and brings Christ's power and authority into the world.

Priest. Priest comes from a Greek word meaning "elder." The priests are coworkers with the bishops; when he is ordained, each priest makes a promise to be obedient to his bishop, and from then on he shares in the apostolic mission of the bishop. Priests bring together all the offerings of the people in the sacrifice of the Mass.

Deacon. The word *deacon* comes from a Greek word meaning "helper." The deacons help by assisting in serving communion, presiding over funerals, and taking care of charitable ministries, among other duties. Deacons are ordained by the bishop's laying his hands on them. Married men may be ordained as deacons in the Western church.

Of course, administering a Church of a billion people requires a more complex organization, so there are divisions within each division.

Some priests serve as the *pastors* of their parishes, helping the other priests direct and administer the affairs of the congregation.

Some bishops serve as *archbishops,* helping to coordinate the affairs of a number of dioceses grouped together in a *province.*

The Bishop of Rome, whom we call the *pope,* as the successor of Peter, has the responsibility of being pastor to the whole Church.

Cardinals are those (usually priests or bishops) who have been chosen for their wisdom and experience to advise and assist the pope, and to choose a new pope when it becomes necessary.

Although the fundamental structure of the Church was set up by Christ himself and his apostles, the Church can make adjustments to the less important forms of its government to keep up with changing times. The pope was not always chosen by the College of Cardinals, for example; in fact, there *wasn't* always a College of Cardinals. But the division of bishops, priests, and deacons will always be with us, because it goes straight back to the New Testament.

IN PRACTICE . . .

In popular culture, priests are almost never treated with respect. They're either figures of fun, or oppressors of the naïve, or — perhaps most commonly — sinister psychopaths. If by rare chance a priest is shown in a sympathetic light, it's usually because he's rebelling against the teachings of the Church.

We know the truth about what a priest is. How can we make the truth heard over the droning chorus of pop culture?

- How do we approach friends who get their whole idea of the priesthood from television and movies?
- What movies or shows can we recommend that show us something like the truth about what a priest is?
- Do I know anyone who might possibly have a vocation to the priesthood? How can I help him discover whether he has that vocation?
- How can we use what we've learned in these sessions to help spread the truth in the darkness?

This is our end-of-study assignment: to go out into the world and be beacons of light. We know what a priest is, and what a miraculous institution the priesthood is. We shouldn't rest until the rest of the world knows, too.

For Further Reading

Acklin, Father Thomas, O.S.B. *The Unchanging Heart of Priesthood.* Steubenville, OH: Emmaus Road, 2006.

Cochini, Christian. *The Apostolic Origins of Priestly Celibacy.* San Francisco: Ignatius Press, 1990.

Dolan, Archbishop Timothy M. *Priests for the Third Millennium.* Huntington, IN: Our Sunday Visitor, 2000.

Grisez, Germain, and Russell Shaw. *Personal Vocation: God Calls Everyone by Name.* Huntington, IN: Our Sunday Visitor, 2003.

Groeschel, Father Benedict, C.F.R. *A Priest Forever: The Life of Father Eugene Hamilton.* Huntington, IN: Our Sunday Visitor, 1998.

Hahn, Scott. *A Father Who Keeps His Promises: God's Covenant Love in Scripture.* Ann Arbor: Servant, 1998.

———. *Many Are Called.* New York: Doubleday (forthcoming, 2010).

———. *Swear to God: The Promise and Power of the Sacraments.* New York: Doubleday, 2004.

Hauke, Manfred. *Women in the Priesthood: A Systematic Analysis in the Light of the Order of Creation and Redemption.* San Francisco: Ignatius Press, 1988.

Heid, Stefan. *Celibacy in the Early Church.* San Francisco: Ignatius Press, 2001.

Stickler, Cardinal Alphonso M. *The Case for Clerical Celibacy: Its Historical Development and Theological Foundations.* San Francisco: Ignatius Press, 1995.

Toups, Father David L., S.T.D. *Reclaiming Our Priestly Character.* Omaha, NE: The Institute for Priestly Formation, 2008.

Wuerl, Most Reverend Donald W. *To Come Follow Me: Reflections on the Ministerial Priesthood.* Pittsburgh: Diocese of Pittsburgh, 2002.

Our Sunday Visitor Web site for the Year for Priests:
www.osv.com/priestyear